THE ANATOMY OF POETRY

By the same author

The Anatomy of Drama
The Anatomy of Language
The Anatomy of Literary Studies
The Anatomy of Prose
The Anatomy of the Novel

THE ANATOMY OF POETRY

by

MARJORIE BOULTON
B.Litt., M.A., D.Phil.

with a foreword by
L. A. G. STRONG

Revised edition

ROUTLEDGE & KEGAN PAUL

LONDON, BOSTON AND HENLEY

First published in 1953
by Routledge & Kegan Paul plc
14 Leicester Square, London WC2H 7PH,
9 Park Street, Boston, Mass. 02108, USA, and
Broadway House, Newtown Road
Henley-on-Thames, Oxon RG9 1EN
Reprinted 1955, 1959, 1962, 1968, 1970,
1974, 1977 and 1979
Second edition revised and reset 1982
Reprinted in 1985
Set in Bembo, 10 on 12pt by
Rowland Phototypesetting, Bury St Edmunds, Suffolk.
Printed in Great Britain by
Thetford Press Limited, Thetford, Norfolk

Library of Congress Cataloguing in Publication Data

Boulton, Marjorie.
The anatomy of poetry.
Bibliography: p.
Includes index.
1. Poetics. I. Title.
PN1042.B6 1982 808.1 82-3651
ISBN 0-7100-9087-0 AACR2

To

HENRY TREECE

the best teacher I ever had

and a most loyal

and understanding friend

CONTENTS

	FOREWORD BY L. A. G. STRONG	ix
	PREFACE	xi
	PREFACE TO THE SECOND EDITION	xv
I	THE IMPORTANCE OF FORM	1
II	THE PHYSICAL FORM OF POETRY	8
III	RHYTHM: (A) METRE	17
IV	RHYTHM: (B) VARIATION: COUNTERPOINT	28
V	PHONETIC FORM: (A) RHYME	45
VI	PHONETIC FORM: (B) ONOMATOPOEIA	58
VII	PHONETIC FORM: (C) INTERNAL PATTERN	65
VIII	FORM IN INTONATION	74
IX	THE USE OF REPETITION: (A) INTELLECTUAL EFFECT	79
X	THE USE OF REPETITION: (B) PURE MAGICAL EFFECT	89
XI	INTELLECTUAL FORM: THE MAIN TYPES OF POETRY	100
XII	INTELLECTUAL FORM: LOGICAL SEQUENCE	112
XIII	INTELLECTUAL FORM: THE USE OF ASSOCIATIONS	124
XIV	INTELLECTUAL FORM: THE TWO MAIN PATTERNS OF IMAGERY	137

XV SOME TRADITIONAL VERSE FORMS 148
XVI FREE VERSE 160
XVII THE CHOICE OF WORDS 168
XVIII TWO POEMS ANATOMIZED 175
XIX HOW NOT TO APPROACH POETRY 185
XX SOME TWENTIETH-CENTURY TECHNIQUES 195
SUGGESTIONS FOR FURTHER READING 217
INDEX 241

FOREWORD

A book about poetry which can be used in the classroom needs first of all to be honest and sensible. This book is very honest and sensible. It is also practical, and written by someone who has never allowed classroom work to dull her original response to poetry.

I am by nature and from experience suspicious of classroom attempts to explain works of art, since they are so often the work of prosaic minds incapable of appreciating anything but rules. Such teachers can comment upon structure and metre, but are insensitive to rhythm, read badly, and never get beyond a strictly rational account of what they think the poem is about. They are of the kind that asks children to paraphrase a poem, and award marks for the result.

This little book is an excellent corrective to any such malpractice. The author shows that it is possible to approach a poem in a business-like manner without spoiling its magic or losing enjoyment of its music. She shows, in fact, that no other approach *is* business-like, since no other will get near the reality of the poem. I do not agree with everything she says, but I commend her book most warmly as a sincere and useful introduction to a great subject; clear-headed, realistic, and easy to understand.

L. A. G. STRONG

PREFACE

I have tried to prevent this from becoming an ill-tempered book, but it was written as the result of prolonged irritation. As a student of literature and later as a teacher in school, emergency training college and three-year training college, as a private coach and lecturing for the W.E.A., I have steadily accumulated exasperation at being unable to find and recommend to my pupils a book on the technique and content of poetry which should be what I wanted them to read. The book I required must be fairly small; it must be more than a string of technical terms yet explain all the usual technical terms; it must have plenty of examples to avoid misunderstanding; it must draw its examples from a wide range of English poetry; it must be up to date, explaining such things as pararhyme and free verse; and, since most of my pupils are trying to take examinations, it must be helpful to the examination candidate without killing poetry by an excess of formalism and pedantry. Never having found such a book, and finding that the appendix on poetry at the back of the grammar book is often too dry to be swallowed, the mass of excellent advanced criticism available to-day rather too rich to be digested by the inexperienced, I have tried to write the book myself and to give an outline of the subject which shall begin at the beginning, but be sufficiently comprehensive on its elementary level. I hope it may be useful to students and teachers.

I should have liked to use more contemporary poetry, but have been deterred by the obstacles of copyright; however, I have tried to encourage the student to read contemporary work. I have made no attempt at giving a potted history of literature such as is readily available elsewhere. This is frankly a technical book, but I have tried to bear in mind that the only sound reason for examining poetry technically is that this adds to our enjoyment.

I have to acknowledge the kindness of Faber & Faber Ltd for permission to quote from W. H. Auden's 'As he is' (in *Collected Shorter Poems*, 1950), and from Louis MacNeice's 'Aubade' (in *Poems*, 1935); of Mr George Fraser for permission to quote from one of his sonnets; of Routledge & Kegan Paul for permission to use a quotation from Sidney Keyes's 'The Wilderness' (in *The Cruel Solstice*, 1944); of Chatto & Windus for permission to quote three extracts from poems by Wilfred Owen from *The Poems of Wilfred Owen*, 1931; and of Mr Robert Penn Warren for permission to quote from his poem 'Original Sin'.

The help I have received in writing this book has really extended over at least the last fifteen years, for all kinds of educational experiences and chance remarks have contributed to it. However, I should like to mention particularly my friends and sometime colleagues, Miss Helen Smith, Miss Freda Sachse, Miss Grace Keenleyside, and Miss Mary Fowler, with all of whom I have had many stimulating discussions on poetry as well as many less bookish pleasures;

my pupils of all ages from eleven to forty-five who have asked me difficult questions and sometimes helped me to knowledge by their alert suggestions, sometimes forced me to clarity by their misunderstandings; my mother, Mrs E. M. Boulton, whose fresh and sincere approach to the arts is an inspiration to me; Mr J. F. Danby, who has given me much mental stimulation and personal encouragement; Allan Jacobs, who read the first draft of this textbook and improved it by a number of penetrating criticisms and thoughtful suggestions. A debt I can never hope to pay is acknowledged in my dedication.

I do not expect that everyone who reads this book will be satisfied; I shall never myself be satisfied with anything I write; but I hope that everyone who reads this book will learn something or be provoked to think.

Stoke-on-Trent
January 1953

PREFACE TO THE SECOND EDITION

I am glad to have had an opportunity to revise and expand this introduction to the study of poetry.

If I were now complacent about a book I wrote thirty years ago, I should show myself so incapable of learning as to be unfit to teach anyone else. With a pile of blank paper before me, I might well, to-day, wish to construct a rather different handbook, bigger, and with different proportions. With a book before me, and a book that numerous students do seem to have found helpful, I welcomed the chance to improve some explanations, supplement some details of information, correct a few correctable faults and provide more varied examples. Any book written thirty years ago about a living art is bound to be out-of-date in some respects; I have tried, as far as its modest scope allows, to remedy this, not only with interpolations, but with a substantial supplementary chapter. Finally, for those readers —I hope, all my readers—for whom my wisdom is insufficient, I have greatly enlarged, updated and particularized the reading-list.

Anyone writing for beginners feels (or should feel) some

tension caused by the opposing pulls of the need to simplify and facilitate, and the duty of not only remembering, but at least hinting to the reader, that hardly anything worth our serious prolonged attention is very simple or penned in rigid certainties. I have at least tried to balance these obligations.

I owe warm thanks for help in preparing this new edition to the admirable staff of the Bodleian Library, to Paul Turner, Dr J. C. Wells, and especially Jean Dukes, who gave most generously of her much occupied time to help me with specialist knowledge.

I hope students will continue to find this book a useful introduction to one of the inexhaustibly interesting great branches of literary studies.

M.B.
Oxford, 1981

I THE IMPORTANCE OF FORM

Form: 1. Relative grouping of the parts of a thing.
WYLD: *Universal Dictionary of the English Language*

The things that are most interesting and most worth having are impossible to define. If we use our common sense, and are careful to say enough, so as to exclude all other objects, we can easily explain what a shovel is, or a telephone, or a bracelet, or even something a little more symbolic such as a sceptre or a pound note. The fact that a man or woman deeply in love can 'find no words' is well known, though the attempt to find words has produced some of our greatest poetry; the fact that the mystic cannot describe intuitive experience accounts in part for the constant arguments on the subject of religion; and hundreds of serious thinkers have been defeated in the attempt to define beauty. Thus, in any analysis which aims at 'explaining' the beauty of poetry, we are to some extent trying to explain the inexplicable.

It does seem, however, that most people agree that one ingredient of beauty is form. Form implies some kind of definiteness or coherence, shape of some kind. A three-tier wedding cake has form, though not usually much beauty; a jelly which has been successfully turned out of a mould has form, though it would be more difficult to describe the exact shape of a moulded jelly than the wedding cake with its three cylinders of different sizes. A cake which has crumbled or been cut into small pieces, a jelly which has failed to set and fallen into an amorphous mass on the dish, lacks form, and although this may be just as digestible and delicious as the geometrical cake or moulded jelly, it is much less attractive to the eye. We appreciate form in such matters as the arrangement of a room or a person's clothes, and dislike an untidy desk or a slovenly person; if we are at all conscious of the artistic possibilities of words, we do not like to hear a speech in which there is no logical sequence or to read a badly written article. Before I began to write this book, I made a plan so that it should at least have form and sequence.

True, some of our most intense, unforgettable experiences of what we feel as beauty seem not to be experiences of organized form: the sight of a vast ocean, a magnificent thunderstorm, snow-veiled woods, the pearl and wool of cloudscapes seen from an aircraft, shimmering golden cornfields, fire, stars. The best moments of life may well be moments of overwhelming passionate tenderness or exalted intuition in which we seem to be not so much deprived of rationality, as liberated from it. Perhaps we do retain some unconscious awareness that nature or emotion at their most apparently limitless are still, like Blake's tiger, obeying laws that are awe-inspiring in their scale and scope? We tend, too, to relish vitality, to admire energy, to be impressed by what seems splendidly greater than ourselves.

Most of the greatest poetry, indeed, treats of great illuminating experiences. Most readers can probably feel that a beautifully organized poem of trivial content, though good, is worth less than one in which profound, lastingly significant matter is organized into an impressive structure.

Anatomy, studied by dissection, is less mysterious and astounding than physiology, the study of the processes of living. Most experiences that can be analysed in an 'Anatomy of Poetry' are experiences of the beauty of form; the purpose of this book is to analyse the things that can be analysed, and a residue that is wonderful and cannot be explained will always be left.

Ideally, no one who is not already well soaked in poetry should attempt close analysis of poems or read literary criticism. First-hand experience should come first. However, all pupils in a classroom cannot be at the same stage of experience; examinations must come at specified times; we cannot always do things in the ideal order.

This book, or any book *about* poetry, is unlikely to give you a healthy appetite for poetry if you do not already have one. Your best medicine will be some book of . . . poems. If you feel you may be missing something by not liking poetry, go and buy or borrow some of the anthologies listed at the end of this book. Dip into them till you feel like reading something steadily; if you find a poem you like, try to read more poems by the same author or similar poems and so try gradually to expand your own capacity for poetry. Perhaps later you will be seized by a curiosity as to how these exciting effects are achieved; that will be the time to read this book and other books on the subject. Of course, if you are taking an examination in English Literature in six months, you had better not leave your textbooks alone till you can approach them in the right spirit; but so long as you know you are, from pressure of circumstances, approaching them in the wrong spirit, you will do yourself no harm.

Or perhaps you like to read poetry for yourself, but

cannot bear to read it aloud or hear it read or recited. You may have heard it mangled and desecrated by little girls with coy squeaks, resentful little boys with raucous shouts or the wrong kind of teacher with soulful mooings. No wonder you feel that poetry brings out the worst in people! Try to listen to poetry readings on radio or television, or first-class records of spoken poetry by such speakers as Richard Burton, Glenda Jackson, Peggy Ashcroft, John Betjeman, T. S. Eliot, Edith Evans and John Gielgud; you will probably have one of the surprises of your life![1]

Ideally, literary criticism ought to arise out of pleasure. What should happen is that we find something delightful and for a time are satisfied with the delight; later, because the healthy mind seldom remains unmoving, we begin to wonder what is the cause of our delight. We may find, rather disconcertingly, that the cause has nothing to do with beauty. You may admire Donne's *Holy Sonnets* because you find them theologically sound, 'edifying'; if so, you may still be unable to see why they are better poetry than *Dare to be a Daniel*. You may like Harold Monro's *Milk for the Cat* because you enjoy the words in their aptness or because you like cats; in the latter situation, a live cat would give you more pleasure. If, however, you read and re-read a poem with pleasure and come to notice that it has an agreeable rhythm, that the sequence of thoughts leads to a climax, that the rhymes are arranged in a pattern which provides reassuring repetitions and stimulating shocks, that the words are more appropriate than any you could put in their place . . . then you are practising the criticism of poetry.

In the early stages of discovering poetry for ourselves, we

[1] Some information about recordings of poetry will be found on pp. 237–9.

often find that to pull it to pieces in any way, even to repeat it to another person, spoils it. Our first worthwhile experience of poetry is very personal, and we feel we want to keep it to ourselves much as we are inclined to be secretive about the beginnings of love in ourselves or about our experience of religion. We may feel that it is almost a profanation to investigate a poem too closely, just as it would be a liberty to be familiar with some person greatly respected. Yet once we have learned to pull poems to pieces intelligently, we find that our pleasure is made deeper by our understanding and the poem is not spoilt. A good poem is more interesting at the twentieth reading than at the first; we can always find something new in it; and, no matter how much we pull it to pieces, as soon as we stand back and look at it the pieces leap together once more.[1]

Readers are often discouraged by the fact that a piece of criticism seems to contain a great many difficult words. Some of them are words which are a stumbling-block to poor spellers; *onomatopoeia* and *alliteration* are among these. There is a reason for the use of these long words. It would be possible to dissect a rabbit and explain our dissection to someone else without using a single recognized anatomical expression; we could make up comprehensible names for ourselves, such as *breath-bags*, *food-bag*, *blood-tubes* and *think-stuff*; yet these terms, being unfamiliar, sound uncouth and childish, and we would actually prefer to use the words that are accepted already. Similarly, a set of defined terms to describe the technique of poetry saves time and misunderstanding. Sometimes it saves too much time, as when a student uses a critical term without knowing the exact

[1] This question of dissection is discussed in more detail in my *The Anatomy of Literary Studies*, chapter 4, pp. 33–41.

meaning, in the hope that it may give the right impression. These terms should be methods of communication and not methods of impressing people with our knowledge. It is as well to learn the critical terms, and a good many will be explained in the course of this book; but what are you to do if you see something in a poem on which you would like to comment, but for which you do not know a special name? Why, simply comment on it in your own words! The proper term would merely make things a little shorter; if you are intelligent enough to be enjoying poetry, you know enough about words to be able to put together some expression for yourself.

We always find something in a poem that we cannot analyse because it exists only in the poem as a whole. If we are trying to understand why a poem delights us, we separate the different parts; the reason for this is the crudely practical one that, though we can perceive several things at once, we cannot describe the several things that we perceive at once, all at the same time; we cannot think two complete sentences simultaneously. When we have separated the various things that go to make a poem what it is, we shall find that one thing is missing; part of the beauty of a poem, part of its form, is the way in which all the component parts are appropriate to each other and fit together. Obviously we cannot analyse this, any more than, when we dissect a rabbit, we can produce its life as a component part. A poem, unlike a rabbit, can be brought to life again after being dissected, but the vital unity can never be adequately defined.

We can usefully distinguish and discuss a number of aspects of form in poetry. The form of poetry is often more obvious than the form of prose, partly because poetry, developed earlier than prose literature and was at first an art of speech or song. The earliest poetry was, so far as we know, social in purpose: the incantation, the rite, the carol, the record of the tribe, the ballad; they were associated with ritual, dance or feasting. Nowadays poetry is often a personal, intimate, even introspective activity, though football chants, greeting cards and protest poems suggest that there is still room in a self-conscious and sceptical society for a social and ritual function of poetry. Poetry, because of its primitive element, has perhaps more obvious physical form than any prose literature. By *physical* I do not of course mean *material*; the *Encyclopaedia Britannica* is a more impressive mass of paper and binding than the *Sonnets* of Shakespeare; I mean that much of the form of poetry can be perceived physically, by the ear and eye, without any intellectual process occurring. Very small children enjoy things that have a marked rhythm, and most of us have had the experience of being captivated by the sound of a poem without fully understanding the words.

In criticism, as often in life, everything is connected with everything else, but to simplify this book I am going to separate the Physical Form and the Intellectual Form of poetry. The Physical Form is the appearance on paper, and, much more important, the sound of poetry. It may be either the sound when poetry is read to us, or the sound we hear mentally when we read it to ourselves. It includes: rhythm, rhyme, intonation and various kinds of echo and repetition. Intellectual Form might be described as Content in the usual sense of the word when applied to literature; it includes: grammatical structure; logical sequence; the pattern of associations; the use of a dominant image; the pattern of image and emotion. All these things combine to give a good poem its power over our imagination.

II THE PHYSICAL FORM OF POETRY

> Untwisting all the chains that ty
> The hidden soul of harmony.
>
> MILTON: *L'Allegro*

It is never possible to distinguish physical form completely from intellectual form, for the two are inter-related. We do not, indeed, know the exact relationship of our physical to our mental being, the extent to which our bodily condition causes our temperament or the exact process by which the mass of stuff known as a brain makes the intangible things called thoughts. Indeed, the mystery of the relationship of physical and intellectual is one of the mysteries that provides material for much art and speculation. Whenever I am trying to explain something quite clearly, I am hindered by an embarrassing awareness that everything is mixed up with everything else. I cannot hope to unmix them completely; I can only try, by means of a few deliberate over-simplifications, to make the study of poetry more comprehensible to the inexperienced reader. When I write about physical and intellectual form, I am not forgetting that as soon as we begin to define the physical form of a poem, we have not merely had a physical experience of it, but have thought about it; when I speak of the intellectual form of a poem, I do not dispute that we hear or read something by means of our ears or eyes, and that this is a physical experience. I hope the reader will also remember these facts, so that he or she is not carrying on a continuous argument with me all through this book!

It is always misleading to separate the physical and intellectual form of a poem so far as to allow ourselves to say: 'What does it mean?' The poem means *itself*; if it could be given to us in a prose paraphrase without losing all its beauty, there would have been no point in writing it as a poem. The poem is a combination of physical and intellectual form and we ought to remember all the time that when we separate these in order to define or discuss them we are no longer discussing the poem. An analogy may be drawn from human personality. What am I? Various people see me as: a woman; a British subject; a Routledge author; an Esperanto poet; a customer; a patient; a close friend; a pest. I am a complicated personality, with a physical existence and a mental existence, both governed by very complex inter-related laws. No such definition is what I 'mean'. A poem, too, has its unique personality, and it is ridiculous to ask what a poem *is* or *means* unless we specify what we, at the moment, want to know about it. It is reasonable to ask what Milton means by:

> Ring out, ye crystal spheres!

if we do not know enough about early astronomy to understand the allusion to the 'crystalline sphere' that was once thought to exist above the visible sky. This is a sensible question that has an answer. But if we take the whole beautiful verse and ask what it means:

Ring out, ye crystal spheres!
Once bless our human ears,
If ye have power to touch our senses so;
And let your silver chime
Move in melodious time;
And let the base of heaven's deep organ blow;
And with your ninefold harmony
Make up full consort to the angelic symphony.

the only proper answer is to repeat the verse again. Later in this book I shall give a few rough prose paraphrases of poems; but they are not, as the reader will see, substitutes for the poems, merely rather dull commentaries to illustrate some point I wish to make. Milton's *Ode on the Morning of Christ's Nativity* is a wonderful poem; we must not ask what it means, but what it feels like when we hear it; it is a fusion of imagination, speculation, learning and masterly verse techniques into one whole which is a work of art.

If another selection of words, a paraphrase, could give the same experience as a poem, there would be no art of poetry. We may, say, explain a rare word, but we cannot divorce the intellectual form, or rather a small part only of the intellectual form (the factual content in its logical sequence) from the totality of the poem, the unique whole that is made up of many mental and physical ingredients. You cannot take an egg out of a cake that has been baked!

When, throughout this textbook, I make distinctions of the various ingredients of poetry, I do so only because it is impossible to talk about two things at once. If I could explain how the various things were fused together to make the whole poem, I should not be a writer of textbooks, but a critical genius.

A rough distinction between sound and sense is perfectly reasonable. There is a real difference between, say, 'The cat sat on the mat' and 'The feline domestic pet was in a seated posture on the small portion of thick fabric'. The stupidest person is conscious of a difference; since the meaning of both statements is the same, the difference must be in the sound. Of this we can say that the first version is shorter and monosyllabic and that, as vowel and consonant are heard three times in the same relationship, it has a kind of crude pattern. This is a (very dull) critical statement about physical form only. Thus we can have two statements with exactly the same meaning but greatly differing in physical form; it would, however, be impossible to have two statements with exactly the same physical form and different meanings, for the fact that certain groups of sounds are assumed to have fixed meanings (or a group of possible meanings) is the basis of language.

Can it be argued that 'You are a beauty!' said in a tone of rapt admiration as by a lover to his lass, and 'You *are* a beauty!' said in an ironical tone by a gardener to a friend who has just plumped a careless foot into a row of seedlings, are two statements with the same physical form but different meanings? No, for the difference in meaning is shown by the intonation, which is immediately perceived by the ear. Everyone who has been to school has at some time heard a poem spoilt by stumbling, mumbling, stupid, or monotonous reading; that a poem can be spoilt by a bad vocal interpretation shows that the intonation is part of the physical form the poet intended. We often find that an argument about the vocal interpretation of a poem may go very deeply into the meaning of a poem.

For a poem to have significant physical form to the eye is

not unknown, though it has never been common in English poetry. (I say *significant*, since everything that is seen, even a beetroot stain on the table-cloth, has *some* form to the eye.) Puttenham, in his *Arte of English Poesie*, 1589—one of the early books in English on the technique of poetry—gives examples of 'shaped poems'. These suggest Puzzle Corner in the newspaper rather than the outpourings of genius, but no doubt provided much harmless and elegant intellectual exercise. In the seventeenth century, George Herbert and Robert Herrick, writers of fine lyrics, also wrote poems which could be fitted into pictorial shapes on the printed page:

The Pillar of Fame

Fame's pillar here, at last, we set,
Outduring marble, brass or jet,
Charm'd and enchanted so
As to withstand the blow
Of overthrow;
Nor shall the seas
Or outrages
Of storms oe'rbear
What we uprear.
Tho' kingdoms fall,
This pillar never shall
Decline or waste at all;
But stand for ever by his own
Firm and well-fixed foundation.

HERRICK

Dylan Thomas has a long and beautiful poem called *Vision and Prayer*, which is shaped on the page into six diamonds and six hourglasses, but also has sound-patterns of great beauty and intricacy. The earliest known shaped poem is a Greek poem in the form of an axe, attributed to Simias, dating from about 300 BC. Interesting though the 'shaped poem' is as a freak, it is not important in the study of poetry. One reason for this is that words of the same length in sound may be of different lengths when printed; a 'shaped poem' is usually a problem for the printer, demanding special spacing. Recent 'Concrete Poetry' may be descended on one side from shaped poems, but is more exciting.[1]

We do, of course, notice the form of a poem on a page when we begin to read. There is a real difference, even visually, between:

For a day and a night Love sang to us, played with us,
Folded us round from the dark and the light;
And our hearts were fulfilled of the music he made with us,
Made with our hearts and our lips while he stayed with us,
Stayed in mid-passage his pinions from flight
For a day and a night.

SWINBURNE: *At Parting*

and

With serving still
This have I won,
For my goodwill
To be undone.

And for redress
Of all my pain
Disdainfulness
I have again.

[1] See pp. 204–8

And for reward
Of all my smart
Lo, thus unheard
I must depart!
WYATT: *His Reward*

As soon as we see these two poems on the page we know that the vocal interpretation will be quite different. Indeed, I think it is safe to say that if they were printed somewhat differently:

For a day and a night
Love sang to us,
Played with us,
Folded us round
From the dark and the light;
And our hearts were fulfilled
Of the music he made with us. . . .

With serving still, this have I won,
For my goodwill to be undone,
And for redress of all my pain,
Disdainfulness to have again. . . .

we should read them aloud somewhat differently, especially the Swinburne; the position of the line-endings is an indication to the reader of the correct vocal interpretation.

Dismissing visual form, however, as relatively unimportant—and, indeed, many of us have our first experience of violent delight in poetry from hearing it read aloud—we find that the physical form of poetry is mainly a pattern of sounds. At the risk, once again, of making false statements by over-simplification or excessive subdivision, we can divide the pattern of sound into two important categories, adding two less important categories. First and most obviously important is rhythm.

As a child, I obediently *ke-bonk, ke-bonked* my pencil on the desk while a teacher, meaning well, grossly misinformed me about the nature of metre, as if Milton's words marched like Cromwell's soldiers. We were taught to force the subtle music of poetry into regular bumpings. Today, I believe, many children are taught nothing at all about metre. Whether total ignorance is better than serious falsification, I am not sure. However, real poetic rhythm is worth studying.

Secondly, there is what I shall allow myself, for want of a better term, to call 'phonetic form'; I refer to patterns made up of resemblances, repetitions or sharp differences of vowel and consonant sounds placed in relation to one another. These too make an important contribution to the music and the emotional effect of poetry.

Thirdly, there is a pattern of intonation, the special emphases dictated by emotion; here, especially, the intellectual form. The thought content, of the poem affects the physical form. Fourthly, various patterns of repetition are obviously a part of both the physical and the intellectual form of a poem. A study of the different uses of repetition will provide our bridge between physical and intellectual form.

A great many poems gain enormously from performance. We ourselves can read poetry silently and drift away in a pleasant mist of words; to try to read it aloud properly forces us to pay full attention to it, to both the music and the meaning, and may well make us understand it for the first time. To hear a poem read aloud by a skilled, sensitive reader may also enormously improve our understanding and appreciation of it. We do well to remember always that poetry began as an oral art and is still to some extent oral.

Any opportunity to hear a living poet read his own work should be taken. It may sometimes be a disappointment; poets presumably hear their own work in their heads, but do not necessarily have the vocal skills to pass on all they hear to an external public; but more often than not it is an exciting, very interesting experience.

III RHYTHM

(A) METRE

'What needs this iterance, woman?'
SHAKESPEARE: *Othello*

We must begin by making a distinction between rhythm and metre; unfortunately textbooks and teachers do not all agree on the correct use of these terms, and the student should always be careful to find out the exact sense in which these words are being used.[1] Both words, when used concerning English poetry, refer to the pattern of stresses. Rhythm I shall take as meaning every possible aspect of this, metre as meaning the symmetrical, repetitive pattern of stresses. Rhythm thus includes metre but metre is a relatively small part of rhythm. The *ke-bonk, ke-bonk* falsification, with its implication that a line not bumping along with unmitigated monotony 'does not scan', must have put many learners off poetry. If poetry really moves in this wooden-legged swing, it is not surprising that many sen-

[1] It is advisable to learn to spell *rhythm*; and in English we write of the *metre* of verse and the *meter* for gas; just to complicate things, Americans have *meter* for verse, and *rime*, which for the English is hoar-frost, for the sound pattern called in English *rhyme*. Examinees should use the spelling accepted in the country in which they are being examined!

sible people do not like it; ordinary speech is so much more varied, subtle and interesting!

English verse rhythm depends upon the arrangement of stresses. There are a number of ways of marking stresses when we are analysing the rhythm of a poem. Some books use the breve (˘) and macron (-), but these are not really suitable for English, as they denote long and short syllables; more will be said about this presently. Some books and teachers use a small cross (x) for an unstressed syllable, and a stroke (/) for a stressed syllable. I was once taught to use an x for an unstressed syllable and an 'a' for a stressed syllable; the disadvantage of this is that it is customary to use letters of the alphabet in describing the pattern of rhymes, and to use letters for both metre and rhyme, e.g. 5xa,ababcc, is rather confusing. As we can assume that if a syllable has not a strong stress it must be a weak stress, it seems reasonable to use a stroke (/) over each stressed syllable, a method used by several good authorities. This has the advantage of not cluttering the page with more symbols than are strictly necessary, and avoids the ugliness of making poetry look like algebra. Thus:

```
       /   /           /      /    /
The cat sat on the mat and ate a rat.
```

clearly indicates which are the stressed syllables. They are simply the ones to which we give more emphasis in natural speech. There are often occasions when I should like a more complicated notation allowing me to indicate both strong and medium stresses as well as unstressed syllables; for instance, in the above sentence the strongest stresses are *cat* and *rat* with *sat, mat* and *ate* as medium-strong or secondary stresses. This, however, would be too detailed for this book, and anyone who can hear at all can hear that some words in a sentence are more important than others.[1]

In English there are two kinds of stress, which are complementary to one another. There is, first, the stress of emphasis. There is a difference between:

/
I want a basket of eggs (not a box)

and

/
I want a basket of eggs (not of oranges).

In two different sentences the same word may be stressed or unstressed, according to its importance:

/ / /
I shall not vote for Mr Fathead, but for Mr Bright.

/ /
I shall not vote for Mr Bright, but I will help him.

The first person is preferring one candidate to another; the second person is presumably under eighteen. Even a usually unimportant word, such as a conjunction or preposition, may on rare occasions carry a strong stress:

/ /
I said, go under the bridge, not over it.

/
Are we allowed a fish course and a meat course here?

[1]More complicated notations have been devised; see the book list.

Common sense enables us to place the natural stress of speech in sentences, whether in poetry or in prose; it should be realized that any stressing of poetry which is contrary to the stressing of normal speech is incorrect. We have to pay attention to the meaning when stressing a sentence, for otherwise we may pass on our misunderstanding to everyone who hears us.

So much for emphatic stress; in words of more than one syllable there is usually one syllable stressed more than the others. English is a very irregular language in this respect, so much so, even, that a word like *contrast* may be stressed differently according to whether it is a noun or a verb, and many words change the position of the stress when a suffix is added. Foreigners often speak 'broken English' by misplacing the stresses, long after they have mastered our difficult grammar and idiom; even educated and intelligent people often stress a word wrongly the first time they meet it. The only certain preventative of such embarrassment is to look the word up in a dictionary before attempting to say it.[1] We habitually say:

/ / / / / /
carpet, kitten, accident, immaterial, retribution

and anyone who said:

/ / / / /
carpet, kitten, accident, immaterial, retribution,

[1] Any good English dictionary gives some indication of how a word should be pronounced, including the stress. The best dictionary for pronunciation only is Daniel Jones: *An English Pronouncing Dictionary*, revised by A. C. Gimson, Dent, 1977.

would immediately be recognized as a foreigner or ignorant. Any interpretation of the rhythm of a poem which forces such a distortion upon a word must be wrong.

The first cultural education given in this country was a classical education in which Latin and Greek were treated as if they were more important than the native tongue. There is much to be said in favour of classical learning, but the extension of its terminology into the study of English literature has done as much harm as good. Languages differ very much in structure; Latin and Greek are highly inflected languages, that is, languages in which the changing endings of words denote their exact grammatical function. English is very little inflected, and depends mainly upon a traditionally correct order of words. Unfortunately, since the study of Grammar in England was originally the study of Latin and Greek grammar, the formal grammar of English is overloaded with Latin terms that do not really suit our language, and, on the other hand, we have no very adequate vocabulary for discussing idiom.

Similarly, the structure of poetry differs in different languages. In English, rhythm depends on stress; in French, the number of syllables is what counts, and English people (including myself) generally put far too much stress into French poetry when reading it aloud. In Greek and Latin verse the pattern is made up of long and short syllables. This is known as *quantity* (a false quantity being the lengthening or shortening of a vowel incorrectly). In English, we cannot really speak of long or short syllables; some vowels are longer than others, other things being equal, so that 'man' is shorter than 'moon', but stress is much more important, and length may be considerably affected by stress: for instance, a vowel in an unstressed syllable frequently becomes a neutral vowel in ordinary rapid speech.[1] Quantitative verse is verse in which the pattern is made by arrangements of long or short syllables. Attempts have been made by poets who were also classical scholars to write English quantitative verse. Examples may be found in the works of Sidney, Spenser, Campion, Tennyson and Clough; but the results have never been encouraging, since no fixed rules for English 'quantities' can be made and we have to read English quantitative verse in a rather artificial manner if the pattern is to be preserved. Such verse can be no more than a technical exercise. For this reason the breve and macron are not at all suitable for the analysis of English rhythms, and all our usual metrical terms, such as *iambic, trochaic* and *dactylic*, being taken from the terminology of quantitative verse, are not ideal for English. Perhaps some day a terminology more suitable to our native tongue will be invented. The sensitive prosodist Robert Bridges tried, without much success, to popularize the terms 'rising' and 'falling' rhythm. The classical terms are not wholly satisfactory, but most of the time work reasonably well, so long as we remember that in scanning English verse we normally use them to denote *stress*, not *quantity*.

When we examine some verses, we notice that a kind of pattern of stresses runs through them. It is not the whole of the rhythm; if this repetitive pattern were the whole, some trivial doggerel for remembering dates might be more 'correct' poetry than most of Milton or Shakespeare; but the pattern is there to be heard. Usually in English two stressed

[1] The best books for any beginner wishing to study the phonetics of English in detail are: J. C. Wells and Greta Colson, *Practical Phonetics*, Pitman, 1971; and J. D. Connor, *Phonetics*, Penguin, 1973.

syllables are separated by at least one unstressed syllable, as we hear in everyday speech:

/ / / / / /
How do you do? I hope you are feeling better to-day?

Stress is produced by putting more force of breath to the syllable. There are not, of course, only two degrees of this force; in a sentence one or two syllables may be very strongly stressed to emphasize important words, while others have some, but less, stress. (In the sentence above, the strongest stress is on *bet-*.) Minor variations of stress must be almost infinite. The *metre* of poetry is *the basic pattern of stressed and unstressed syllables.*

If a line of poetry begins with a stressed syllable, the pattern will run something thus:

/ / / /
Minnehaha, Laughing Water. . . .

or, perhaps:

/ /
Take her up tenderly,
/ /
Lift her with care. . . .

and the effect will be 'falling', as Bridges calls it. The first pattern is called TROCHAIC, and may be described as alternating stressed and unstressed syllables, beginning with a stressed syllable. The second is called DACTYLIC, and may be described as alternating one stressed and two unstressed syllables, beginning with a stressed syllable. (Those who knit will know that when we are doing 'knit one, purl one' it does matter very much whether we begin the row with a knit or purl stitch.) It will be noticed that in the example of dactylic pattern chosen there is a stressed syllable at the end of the second line, without the two unstressed syllables that might be expected. This omission of final unstressed syllables often happens in the two main 'falling' rhythms, since there are relatively few English words that would fit the complete rhythm. More will be said about these variations, often wrongly called irregularities, in the next chapter.

The commonest kind of English metre has a pattern something like this:

/ / / / /
That time of year thou may'st in me behold. . . .

—a pattern alternating stressed and unstressed syllables beginning with an unstressed syllable. This is called IAMBIC. It is found, with five stresses to a line, in all the plays of Shakespeare, all heroic couplets, all sonnets, *Paradise Lost, The Faerie Queene, Idylls of the King* and many more of our best-known poems; iambic metre is also the basis of many other well-known English verse forms. As it happens, the commonest variation in iambic verse is to invert the order of the stresses in the first group, so the student who is looking for iambic rhythm should be careful to pick it up by ear rather than by arithmetic. Even in the line above, chosen for its regularity, I am not at all sure that it might not be better to put the stress on the first rather than the second word.

The last metre that is at all common in English is the ANAPAESTIC, a pattern in which one stressed syllable alternates with two unstressed syllables, but beginning with the two unstressed syllables, as:

/ / / /
The Assyrian came down like a wolf on the fold. . . .

It will be noticed that this gives a feeling of urgent movement.

Certain other terms borrowed from classical prosody are sometimes used in describing English verse, but, though such feet are occasionally found in English, whole lines in these patterns are extremely rare. These are: Spondee (two stressed syllables together), Amphibrach (unstressed-stressed-unstressed), Amphimacer or Cretic (stressed-unstressed-stressed) and Pyrrhic (two unstressed). Amphibrachic lines are found in limericks; there are a number of spondaic lines in W. H. Davies's *School's Out*.

When we analyse the basic pattern or *metre* of a poem, we first decide upon the basic pattern (iambic, trochaic, anapaestic or dactylic) and then divide it into FEET to give the type of line. The safest way to divide a line into feet is to count the stressed syllables first; in the basic pattern there are as many feet as stressed syllables, and the 'foot' is the stressed syllable together with the unstressed syllables that naturally attach themselves to it. (If there seem to be some syllables 'left over', they should probably be 'left over' at the end of the line rather than at the beginning.) Scansion, however, is a matter of cultivating the ear rather than learning fixed rules, for the basic pattern is never found for long without variations, and the student who tries to treat scansion as an aspect of arithmetic is sure to be seriously misled sooner or later.

The number of feet in a line is important. Obviously, a short line has fewer feet than a long one. For those who like a lot of technical terms, or are expected to make use of them, here are the terms for lines of various lengths:

Seven feet (very rare)	SEPTENARIUS
Six feet	HEXAMETER (This is also the name of a common classical metre.)
Five feet (our commonest line)	PENTAMETER
Four feet	TETRAMETER (*not* Quadruped!)
Three feet	TRIMETER
Two feet	DIMETER
One foot (rare)	MONOMETER.

Thus in the examples given above the first is TROCHAIC TETRAMETER, the first line of the second a DACTYLIC DIMETER, the third example an IAMBIC PENTAMETER, and the fourth an ANAPAESTIC TETRAMETER. These terms sound very dull, but it is sometimes convenient to know them.[1]

Here are six little helps to memory for the student who is liable to confuse the main basic English metres:

Iambic feet are firm and flat
And come down heavily like THAT.

Trochees dancing very lightly
Sparkle, froth and bubble brightly.

Dactylic daintiness lilting so prettily
Moves about fluttering rather than wittily.

While for speed and for haste such a rhythm is the best
As we find in the race of the quick anapaest.

Bigfoot Spondee thumps down,
Stone slab, dead weight, lead crown.

[1] May an experienced examiner warn readers that all the words describing the number of feet in a line end in -METER, and that the basic pattern is METRE?

There came an old Amphibrach tripping,
And fell in a basin of dripping.

When we have learned to recognize these customary basic patterns, we may be tempted to think that we know all about the rhythm of poetry. In fact, the most interesting part, which is yet to come, is more important and is often ignored.

IV RHYTHM

(B) VARIATION: COUNTERPOINT

> Change is the nursery
> Of musicke, joy, life and eternity.
>
> DONNE: *Elegy III*

If we try to work out the rhythm of a poem merely by counting syllables, tapping our fingers on the table or repeating the lines in the monotonous and murderous *ke-bonk, ke-bonk* fashion, we shall soon find ourselves in difficulties. Let us take a favourite line from Shakespeare:

To be or not to be, that is the question. . . .

We may think (rightly) that Shakespeare's basic verse pattern was the iambic pentameter, and, ke-bonking happily on the desk, produce the following monstrosity:

```
    /     /      /       /       /
To be or not to be, that is the question.
```

If we know our technical terms, we then say that this is a regular iambic pentameter line except for one extra unstressed syllable at the end. The scholar may object that there are probably two unstressed syllables at the end, as -ion endings were often pronounced i-on in Shakespeare's day. This does not much matter; but if we try to speak the line as our mechanical stresses indicate, we soon realize that it is completely unnatural and very ugly. A Hamlet who talked thus would be pelted off the stage. If we stress the line as the thought in it suggests, it will probably be something like this:

/ / / /
To be or not to be, that is the question

with rather less stress on 'quest-' than on the other stressed syllables. *What* is troubling Hamlet is the problem of whether to *live* or to *die*; these, the important ideas, should dictate the stresses.

If we turn back to the example of dactylic metre in Chapter III, we find:

/ /
Take her up tenderly,

/ /
Lift her with care.

The first line is 'regular'; in the second, we have a dactylic foot of perfect 'regularity' followed by a single stressed syllable. To speak of this as an 'irregularity', as if it were a carelessness on the part of the poet, is stupid; carelessness would be ugly. The effect of this is beautiful and adds to the feeling of gentle regret, the 'dying fall' suitable to the pathetic theme of a young girl's suicide. Dactylic metre in English generally has some incomplete feet, as the number of dactylic words in English is small, and, if the line is to end with a rhyme-word, a whole word is needed for the last foot, rather than a monosyllable followed by two unimportant words. In classical prosody a line which has an 'extra' syllable or syllables is called a line with *hypermetric* syllables and a line which has a syllable short is called *catalectic*. It is also possible for a whole foot to be *hypermetric*. These terms can be applied to English versification and the student may find it convenient to be able to recognize them, though there is probably no need to make the effort to learn them.

If we take the line from *Hamlet* as it is stressed in natural speech, according to the meaning, we must describe it something like this:

> 'Iambic pentameter, with an unstressed third foot, inversion of the fourth foot and one or possibly two hypermetric syllables after the last foot.'

We might add, if we were being very minute in our description:

> 'The strongest stress in the line is on the stressed syllable of the inverted fourth foot.'

'Regularity,' in the sense of each foot being exactly like the next and each line being exactly like the next, would be not a merit but a defect in poetry. Most people not poets, when they try to write verses, find it difficult to make them 'scan' unless they have a natural ear for rhythm, but a series of completely 'regular' lines would be, not a proof of poetic skill, but unbearably monotonous.

Rather than vandalize a good poem, I have composed a bit of verse and made it dead regular:

/ / / / /
It rains and rains and rains and rains and rains.

/ / / / /
The children fret and Tib the cat complains.

/ / / / /
The washing hangs around the living-room;
/ / / / /
The sky is solid grey, a dome of gloom;
/ / / / /
We have to leave our shoes to block the door,
/ / / / /
Or muddy marks will mess the shining floor;
/ / / / /
We'd like a cake for tea, but no one feels
/ / / / /
Inclined to go, and get as wet as eels,
/ / / / /
In minutes, dashing down to seek the shop.
/ / / / /
O sun, do shine; do tell this rain to stop.

There are five stresses in each line, arranged with mathematical regularity, though exact equality is not possible—'eels' clearly has more stress than 'get', and so on. The result makes sense, but sounds sing-song and rather dull. Let us now see what happens when, keeping the same set of ideas, I adjust these iambic pentameters to provide variety. The first two lines can be kept regular: that sets a pattern, and the first line suggests the monotony of the rain:

/ / / / /
It rains and rains and rains and rains and rains.

/ / / / /
The children fret and Tib the cat complains.

/ / / / / / Wet washing decorates the living-room;	a strong first foot adds emphasis; the weakish third foot may suggest irony and exasperation?
/ / / / / / / Dead grey lead sky lies a low dome of / gloom;	three strong feet and one inverted foot give a very heavy line.
/ / / / / Shoes sprawl, a hindering heap beside the / door,	a strong first foot adds emphasis and if the 'er' in 'hindering' does get sounded in the reading, the rhythm almost suggests tripping up!
/ / / / Lest muddy marks should mess the shining / floor.	Back to basic pattern again.
/ / / / / We'd like a cake for tea, but no-one wishes	hypermetrical syllable at end gives feminine rhyme.
/ / / / / To do the errand, getting wet as fishes	ditto
/ / / / / In just five minutes, going to the shop.	strong second foot, compensated by weak fourth.
/ / / / / Shine, sun! Command this soaking rain to / stop.	strong first foot gives a dramatic emphasis.

The reader can, I hope, see and hear that the rhythm is now more natural and lively. Though less regular, it is now in fact more artistic, with meaningful emphases, more care to have the sound fitting the meaning, and a faintly amusing surprise in the feminine rhyme. To think about such things demands appreciably more skill and sensitivity than to commit *kebonk*ery.

Shakespeare uses variations with genius instead of crudity, as in the lovely, haunting line:

/   /   /   /   /   /
Bare ruined choirs, where lȧte the sweet birds sang.

There is also a lighter stress on 'birds', making the line a very heavy and melancholy one.

It will be seen from the above examples that the main possibilities of varying the basic metre of a poem are: leaving one foot without its expected stress; putting two strong stresses in one foot; putting a hypermetric syllable at the end of a line or elsewhere; inverting any foot. These variations can be practised on all four usual basic metres.

The function of the basic metre is to provide a regular undercurrent, a kind of pulse-beat of the poem, over which the interesting variations are heard. Unless we recognize the basic metre, by ear at least, not necessarily by name, we cannot appreciate the variations. What happens when we hear a poem and like the rhythm is that we quickly (probably after the first line) learn to expect a repetition of this pattern; we keep receiving small shocks of different kinds, which are pleasurable. At least, they are pleasurable in the work of a good poet! If they are not, we are roused to protest that the verses 'do not scan'. It is most unfortunate that many people have had so narrow a concept of 'rhythm' forced upon them that they feel a poem 'does not scan' if it contains variations, and therefore try to force it into unnatural, ugly rhythms if it is the work of an acknowledged master, or condemn it as incompetent if it is by a living poet who has not yet established a reputation. Readers with more musical talent than I have can pursue further the idea that these variations on basic metre are comparable with counterpoint, descant or syncopation in various kinds of music. Other analogies may be drawn from our everyday experience. In marriage, a husband or wife is expected to be faithful, loyal and reliable; but marriages in which routine is all-important and neither spouse ever seeks to give a pleasant surprise to the other, or there is no spontaneity or fun, are not very successful. We wish to have steady, trustworthy friends; we take pleasure in their habits and customs, their personal repetitions, but we all like to have friends who are also interesting and sometimes surprise us with original ideas, or do unusual things. We enjoy going for a walk along the same lane many times; but, while part of the pleasure is in the familiarity, part lies in the new discoveries at different seasons and in different weathers. It could well be argued that all personal life, all human history, consists of basic patterns on which variations are superimposed. In skilfully written poetry, the variations on the basic metre generally coincide with important words or with changes of emotion. Shakespeare is full of magnificent examples of this; the marriage of metrical to emotional change is obviously more valuable in dramatic even than in lyrical poetry.

When Romeo is about to poison himself over what he believes to be the dead body of Juliet, he says:

O! here
Will I set up my everlasting rest
And shake the yoke of inauspicious stars
From this world-wearied flesh. Eyes, look your last!

In this last line there are two stresses in the fourth foot, emphasizing Romeo's resolve to die and making the pathos of the last farewell more solemn. Another beautiful effect achieved by the variation of the fourth foot is to be found in *The Winter's Tale*, this time in a happy context. Hermione meets her daughter, Perdita, who has been lost for sixteen years. She greets her thus:

> You gods, look down
> And from your sacred vials pour your graces
> Upon my daughter's head! Tell me, mine own,
> Where hast thou been preserved?

How tender and urgent in its emphasis is that inverted fourth foot, 'Tell me . . .'. To stress the basic pattern here and say 'Tell *me*' would be obviously absurd, since no one else is asking Perdita to tell her story.

Out of weakness, too, a line can be made strong; one of the strongest lines in *Othello* has only three stressed syllables, thus throwing great emphasis on to those syllables:

```
            /           /      /
It is the cause, it is the cause, my soul!
```

At the other end of the scale, Milton makes one line from *Paradise Lost* heavy and impressive by loading with stressed syllables:

```
  /      /      /      /    /     /       /
Rocks, Caves, Lakes, Fens, Bogs, Dens, and shades

      /
  of Death,
```

in which lines the first three feet are spondees!

In a lighter context, Viola in *Twelfth Night* says:

None of my lord's ring! why, he sent her none!

where the inversion of the first foot emphasizes 'none' and suggests an intonation of surprise; the two stresses in the third foot clash together; she is answering her own question. In *Much Ado about Nothing*, when Leonato is outraged by the supposed unchastity of his innocent daughter, he says fiercely:

For, did I think thou wouldst not quickly die,
Thought I thy spirits were stronger than thy shames,
Myself would, on the rearward of reproaches,
Strike at thy life. Griev'd I, I had but one?

The first line is more or less 'regular'; the next line has a hypermetric syllable, and this time it is not at the end of the line, which is a firm monosyllable of emphatic meaning, but must be taken as the second syllable of either 'spirits' or 'stronger'; this stumble in the middle of the line helps to suggest Leonato's mental distress. The next line has another hypermetric syllable, this time at the end; the second and fourth feet are both inverted, making a very loose line; this leads up to the shock of the next foot, 'Strike at', which is inverted to give it additional force. In this line we then have an inversion of the third foot which emphasizes 'Griev'd'. We can take any play of Shakespeare's at random and speedily find a number of interesting examples of the way in which these variations, standing out in contrast to an underlying basic pattern, give dramatic point and emphasis to particular words. Indeed, some of Shakespeare's acknowledged superiority to his contemporaries lies in his use of rhythm for dramatic purposes. For instance, almost all Marlowe's lines, even in his finest passages, are stopped at the end; Shakespeare's, in which the sense of one line frequently runs over into the next, are more flexible.[1] If we read Shakespeare's plays in approximate chronological order, we see how he moved away from the end-stopped line to a more flexible line. The dramatists of the Jacobean period are even more flexible in their verse rhythms, so much so that they sometimes lose the basic pattern and stumble into a kind of half-verse, half-prose. Here is a passage from Webster's *The Duchess of Malfi* in which the variations add to the pathos:

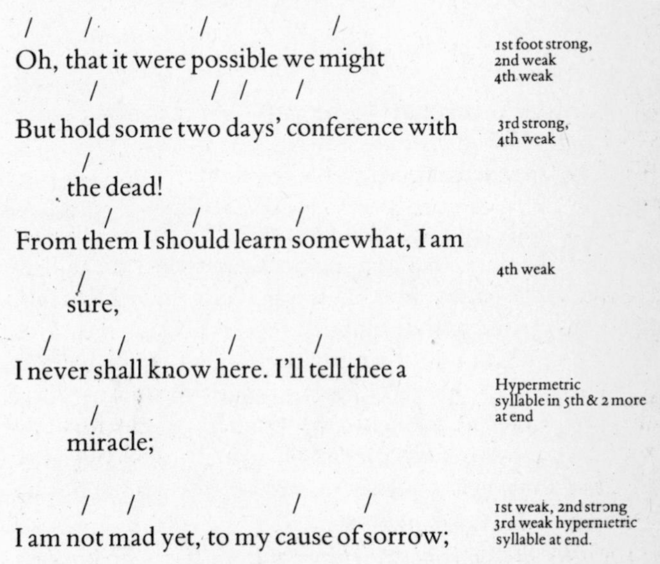

[1] The technical term for a line in which the end of the metrical line coincides with a pause in the sense is *end-stopped*. If the sense carries straight over into the next line, the line is *enjambé* and the technique is *enjambement*.

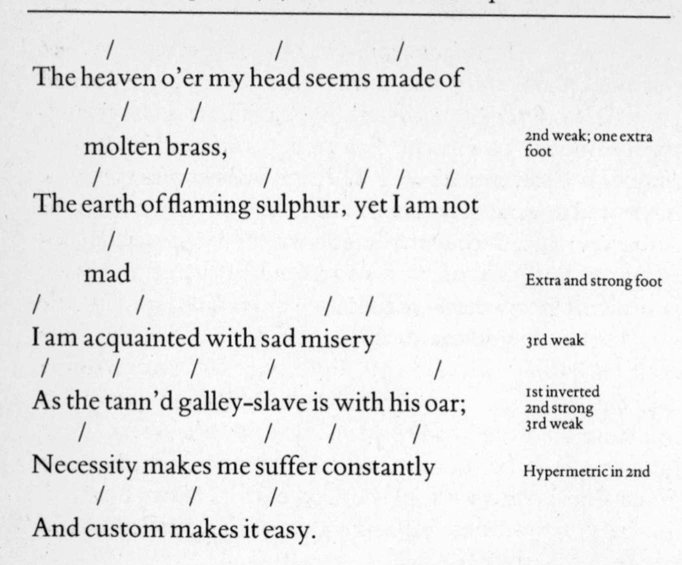

The heaven o'er my head seems made of
molten brass, — 2nd weak; one extra foot
The earth of flaming sulphur, yet I am not
mad — Extra and strong foot
I am acquainted with sad misery — 3rd weak
As the tann'd galley-slave is with his oar; — 1st inverted, 2nd strong, 3rd weak
Necessity makes me suffer constantly — Hypermetric in 2nd
And custom makes it easy.

This play was first published in 1623. In this passage there is so much variation that at times we seem to lose the under-current of the iambic beat. This might elsewhere be a fault; variation carried to the point that there is nothing on which to have a variation is obviously useless; but in this context the looseness of the verse has a strange, touching beauty; after long mental torment, the Duchess is still resisting madness, and the touch of verbal and metrical incoherence suggests how near to it she has come; the madmen who enter presently speak in prose.

Here I will mention the *Theory of Equivalence*, an import-ant development in the history of English prosody, and one to which the student may find allusions. It is also sometimes called the *Theory of Substitution*, and is another way of expressing what I have been trying to explain, depending rather more on those concepts of classical prosody which are no longer a part of the information of every educated person. It is discussed in detail, with a rich store of interesting examples, in George Saintsbury's *Manual of English Prosody*, a book which every student who becomes seriously interested in verse forms ought to read. (It is rather solid for an inexperienced student.) According to the theory of substitution, one kind of foot may be substituted for another equivalent foot; an iambic foot may be replaced somewhere in a line by a trochaic or anapaestic foot, a trochaic foot replaced by a dactyl and so on; it must not take place so often that the basic metre is lost. Even Saintsbury, with his immense erudition, had to admit that the experience of the human ear, rather than a fixed rule, showed whether in a given line a substitution was acceptable. What I call an 'inverted iambic foot' Saintsbury would have called a 'substituted equivalent trochee'.

So far we have studied metre and variation chiefly in dramatic blank verse. Variation will be more common in the best dramatic verse than in non-dramatic verse, because, as I hope I have shown, it plays a part in the actual dramatic effect. However, examples may be found throughout the mass of English lyric poetry. Here are a few lines from Andrew Marvell's *The Garden*:

> How vainly men themselves amaze
> To win the palm, the oak, or bays,
> And their incessant labours see
> Crowned from some single herb or tree,
> Whose short and narrow-verged shade
> Does prudently their toils upbraid;
> While all flowers and all trees do close
> To weave the garland of repose.

The first two lines are completely 'regular', to enable the reader to grasp the basic pattern of iambic tetrameter. The first foot in the third line is weak, leading up effectively to the stress on 'Crowned', an emphatic inversion. The next conspicuous variation is in line 7, an oddly beautiful line in its rhythmical context. I think it should be scanned:

/ / / / /
While all flowers and all trees do close.

Here we have two feet inverted, or two substituted equivalent trochees, with a strange effect of wonder in the natural intonation. In the next line there is only one inversion.

Often in lyrical poetry, especially short lyrics, substitution or variation is such that the effect is of a mixed metre. This is not the mere loss of the basic metre in confusion, which would sound like bad prose and be slovenly writing, but must, I think, be taken as an example of what is common in classical metres, a basic line pattern made up of more than one kind of foot. A pretty example is the well-known song from John Gay's *Acis and Galatea*:

O ruddier than the cherry,
O sweeter than the berry,
O Nymph more bright
Than moonshine night,
Like kidlings blithe and merry.
Ripe as the melting cluster,
No lily has such lustre,
Yet hard to tame
As raging flame
And fierce as storms that bluster.

The basic metre of this poem would seem, if we look at the four short lines, to be iambic, but in all the other lines, though the basis is iambic, the last foot has a hypermetric syllable making a feminine rhyme. This is so much a part of the structure that the basic metre of the poem might be said to be iambic-plus-trochaic, or perhaps, from the terminology of Bridges, a rising rhythm with a falling conclusion. Perhaps this is being over-pedantic, but I think we should have a distinction between sporadic and systematic variation. Perhaps if we had not taken all our metrical terms from the classics we should have found a better way of expressing this!

A student working with me was once greatly puzzled by the rhythm of Tennyson's *Break, break, break*. The reader should have a try before looking at my analysis, as a test! Here is the poem with the lines numbered for easy reference later:

1 Break, break, break
2 On thy cold gray stones, O sea!
3 And I would that my tongue could utter
4 The thoughts that arise in me.

5 O well for the fisherman's boy,
6 That he shouts with his sister at play!
7 O well for the sailor lad,
8 That he sings in his boat on the bay!

9 And the stately ships go on
10 To their haven under the hill;
11 But O for the touch of a vanished hand
12 And the sound of a voice that is still!

13 Break, break, break,
14 At the foot of thy crags, O Sea!
15 But the tender grace of a day that is dead
16 Will never come back to me.

We can probably hear a pattern in this poem long before we can say what the basic metre is. It is one of those poems in which the rhythm is so delicate and complex that any attempt to *ke-bonk* it into a regular pattern would mislead more than in a more regular poem. It is necessary to read the poem aloud, intelligently, and mark the syllables that are naturally stressed, remembering that equal stress is not laid on all stressed syllables. The basic metre of this poem is anapaestic, strange as this may seem in view of its slow, melancholy rhythm. Completely regular anapaestic trimeters are found in lines 6, 8, and 12, and nearly regular ones with only one unstressed syllable missing in lines 5, 10, and 14. Lines 11 and 15 also have unmistakably the anapaestic beat, but each, a tetrameter, has one iambic foot. Eight puzzling lines remain: the two pathetic repetitions of 'Break, break, break . . .' I would read as three almost equal strong stresses, making a very heavy line for the mood of mourning. Lines 2, 4, 7, and 16, have each three stresses, with a mixture of iambic and anapaestic feet. The effect of these complicated variations is to give a faltering effect to the poem, which well suggests by its sound the emotion it portrays.

Tennyson was a brilliant conscious artist. William Blake was a spontaneous rather than a subtle prosodist; believing his poems to be literally and directly inspired, he seldom polished them as most poets do. Here is a short poem of indisputable beauty and power, which is, however, as enigmatic rhythmically as symbolically:

/ /
O Rose, thou art sick!

/ /
The invisible worm

/ /
That flies in the night

/ /
In the howling storm,

/ /
Has found out thy bed

/ /
Of crimson joy

/ / / /
And his dark secret love

/ /
Does thy life destroy.

This poem is almost too short to give us the sense of expectation that a basic metre would provide. It begins with three lines in the same rhythm, an iambic foot (with a slur in line 2, 'Th' in . . .') followed by an anapaest; the order is then reversed for two lines; an iambic dimeter follows; the eighth line is an anapaest with an iambic foot; the seventh line is anything but easy to describe. It seems to me to have four stresses, closely packed and sinister in tone. This poem implies by its very rhythm a kind of profoundly wise naïvety, although the suitability of the rhythm may not be calculated.

Many more examples could be cited for all our purposes, but perhaps enough have been discussed to show that the rhythms of poetry are not a matter of tapping mechanically on a desk or counting syllables on our fingers. Quite often it is possible to have a difference of opinion, not only on how the arrangement of stresses in a poem should be described, but on where the actual stresses are to be placed; otherwise the only differences in the interpretation of poems when spoken by different people would lie in the quality of the voices, and it is common experience that this is not so. Indeed, a certain ambiguity of rhythm is one of the beauties of a poem. Sincerity is as important in the study of rhythm as in any other literary study, and any attempt to force the words into a too symmetrical pattern outrages the healthy ear.

V PHONETIC FORM

(A) RHYME

> Where'er you find *the cooling western breeze*,
> In the next line, it *whispers through the trees*;
> If crystal streams *with pleasing murmurs creep*,
> The reader's threaten'd (not in vain) with *sleep*.
>
> POPE: *An Essay on Criticism*

Some years ago I was walking along a country lane with a friend; we were trying to string some verses together; and my friend, who had a lively mind but no talent for verse composition, struggled with a promising first line until, giving up in despair, she convulsed us both by exclaiming: 'But I can't get a worm to ride!'

'A worm to ride' is the first thing the beginner in verse-writing seeks and the most obvious part of the physical form of poetry. Rhyme is a repetition of some arrangement of vowels and consonants at the ends of lines, or sometimes in the middle, and is defined by H. W. Fowler in *Modern English Usage* as 'identity of sounds between words or lines extending back from the end to the last fully accented vowel and not farther'. Thus a rhyme-word may in theory have one, two, three, four or more syllables, though in practice, in serious poetry, rhymes of more than two syllables are rare. One-syllable rhymes may be called *masculine*, though there is seldom any need for the term; two-syllable rhymes, e.g. nation-station, are called *feminine*. If we wish to describe any other kind of rhyme we can use the words *trisyllabic* and *polysyllabic*, or *triple* and *quadruple*.

The student who has read attentively so far will see that feminine rhymes may be expected in trochaic verse or as a variation (a last foot with a hypermetric syllable) in iambic verse; masculine rhymes will be found in iambic verse or as variations (catalectic) in trochaic verse. Many different arrangements of rhymes are possible, from the extreme simplicity of the old ballads:

> I'll do as much for my true love
> As any young man may;
> I'll sit and mourn all at her grave
> For a twelvemonth and a day.

to the extreme elaboration of, say, Spenser's *Prothalamion*:

> Calm was the day, and through the trembling air
> Sweet-breathing Zephyrus did softly play
> A gentle spirit, that lightly did delay
> Hot Titan's beams, which then did glister fair;
> When I (whom sullen care,
> Through discontent of my long fruitless stay
> In Prince's court, and expectation vain
> On idle hopes, which still do fly away,
> Like empty shadows, did afflict my brain.)
> Walked forth to ease my pain.
> Along the shore of silver streaming Thames;
> Whose rutty bank, the which his river hems,
> Was painted all with variable flowers,
> And all the meads adorned with dainty gems

Fit to deck maidens' bowers
And crown their paramours
Against their bridal day, which is not long:
Sweet Thames! run softly till I end my song.

It is customary and convenient to denote patterns of rhyme (commonly called 'rhyme-schemes') briefly by using letters of the alphabet; thus, the first example may be described as abcb and the second as abbaabcbccddedeeff. (We might also describe the first as abab; the matter of imperfect rhyme will be discussed later.) A detailed account of the common English rhyme-schemes with their usual names will be found in Chapter XV; though the student should not become obsessed with technical terms as if they were the most important part of appreciation.

The rhyme-scheme of a poem plays a part in its emotional effect, though not generally so great a part as the rhythm. The elaborate rhyme-scheme of Spenser's *Prothalamion* in itself suggests something formal, ceremonious and processional. Narrative is usually written in some fairly simple rhyme-scheme, such as the couplet (many of Chaucer's *Canterbury Tales*, Keats's *Lamia*, Scott's *Marmion*, Shelley's *The Sensitive Plant* and Byron's *The Prisoner of Chillon*) or the simple quatrain rhyming abcb or abab, as in the old ballads and later imitations of them such as Coleridge's *The Ancient Mariner.*[1] Sometimes, however, a more elaborate verse form is used for narrative, the most remarkable example being the difficult nine-line Spenserian stanza used in Spenser's *The Faerie Queene*; other complicated stanza

[1] The latter poem has also some internal rhymes and variations on the rhyme-scheme; these are occasionally found in the old ballads.

forms for narrative may be found in Keats's *Isabella*, Byron's *Don Juan*, Shelley's *The Revolt of Islam* and many of the narrative poems of Robert Browning. A narrative using one of the more complicated verse forms will move more slowly, in general, than one in a simpler form; it will contain less action and more description or reflection.

Satire demands a crisp rhyme-scheme, in which the unkind remarks follow one another rapidly, without fumbling. Heroic couplets, that is iambic pentameter couplets, are a favourite form for satire, as in Byron's *The Age of Bronze*:

> The *landed interest*—(you may understand
> The phrase much better leaving out the *land*)
> The land self-interest groans from shore to shore
> For fear that plenty should attain the poor.
> Up, up, again, ye rents! exalt your notes,
> Or else the ministry will lose their votes,
> And patriotism, so delicately nice,
> Her loaves will lower to the market price.

Thousands of different rhyme-schemes are possible for short lyrics, depending on the mood; alternations of long and short lines add to the variety. A very short lyric may not repeat a rhyme-scheme at all, but be, as it were, one verse; many of the Elizabethan madrigals are like this:

> Faustina hath the fairer face,
> And Phillida the feater grace;
> Both have mine eye enriched.
> This sings full sweetly with her voice,
> Her fingers make as sweet a noise;
> Both have mine ear bewitched.

Ay me! sith Fates have so provided,
My heart, alas! must be divided.
ANONYMOUS, from *Airs and Madrigals*, 1598

More often a short poem repeats a verse form once, if only once:

When to her lute Corinna sings,
Her voice revives the leaden strings,
And doth in highest notes appear
As any challenged echo clear.
But when she doth of mourning speak,
Even with her sighs the strings do break.

And as her lute doth live or die,
Led by her passion, so must I.
For when of pleasure she doth sing,
My thoughts enjoy a sudden spring;
But if she doth of sorrow speak,
E'en from my heart the strings do break.
THOMAS CAMPION

The actual repetition of the verse form is part of the symmetry of a poem, and has perhaps something the same effect as parallelism in prose, as in 'He hath put down the mighty from their seats, and He hath exalted the humble and meek'.

The vast majority of English poems until the twentieth century have rhymes of one syllable, if they rhyme at all, blank verse (unrhymed iambic pentameter) having long been a favourite English form. Feminine rhymes, less common, trip rather more lightly:

Trip no further, pretty sweeting;
Journeys end in lovers meeting!

Poets quite often use masculine and feminine rhymes in alternation; this generally seems to produce a very melodious verse. Swinburne, a poet of more music than meaning at times, particularly favours this kind of rhyme-scheme:

From too much love of living,
From hope and fear set free,
We thank with brief thanksgiving
Whatever gods may be
That no life lives for ever;
That dead men rise up never;
That even the weariest river
Winds somewhere safe to sea.
The Garden of Proserpine

Thomas Hood uses an alternation of masculine and trisyllabic rhyme in the poem quoted in the third chapter:

Take her up tenderly,
Lift her with care;
Fashioned so slenderly,
Young, and so fair!
The Bridge of Sighs

Feminine rhymes are often used in humorous verse, in which they please by their witty ingenuity. The delight here is probably almost entirely in the pleasant shock of the unexpected. We wonder how the writer can possibly find a rhyme to the line we have just heard; but no—here it comes! The Puritans in Samuel Butler's *Hudibras*:

Compound for sins they are inclined to
By damning those they have no mind to

Quarrel with minced-pies, and disparage
Their best and dearest friend, plum-porridge;

Shall I borrow the wand of a Moorish enchanter,
And bid a decanter contain the Levant, or
The brass from the face of a Mormonite ranter?
Shall I go for the mule of the Spanish Infantar—
(That *r*, for the sake of the line, we must grant her,)—
And race with the foul fiend, and beat in a canter,
Like that first of equestrians Tam o'Shanter?

C. S. CALVERLEY

Rhymes of more than two syllables are very seldom used except with humorous intention, for they are so ingenious that we notice them as rhymes as well as an integral part of the verse form. Byron uses a good many multiple rhymes in *Don Juan*:

Some women use their tongues—she *look'd* a lecture,
Each eye a sermon, and her brow a homily,
An all-in-all sufficient self-director,
Like the lamented late Sir Samuel Romilly,
The Law's expounder, and the State's corrector,
Whose suicide was almost an anomaly—
One sad example more than 'All is vanity'—
The jury brought their verdict in 'Insanity'.

W. S. Gilbert often used comic multiple rhymes, e.g.

Then I can write a washing bill in Babylonic cuneiform,
And tell you every detail of Caractacus's uniform.

When, in *Much Ado about Nothing*, Benedick is trying to write a love poem, he can think of no rhyme for 'school' but 'fool'; in *Romeo and Juliet* Mercutio invites Romeo to 'rhyme me but love and dove', so in Shakespeare's day poets were already aware that some rhymes were hackneyed. The number of full rhymes to any word is limited. In humorous verse imperfect rhymes are cheerfully accepted, as in Byron's

> Whereas, if one sole lady pleased for ever,
> How pleasant for the heart, as well as liver!

and a few rhymes which are rhymes to the eye rather than the ear, such as *love* and *move*, have long been permitted by convention. Poets recognized as fine craftsmen, writing seriously, have sometimes allowed themselves imperfect rhymes:

> Her weed she then withdrawing did him discover;
> Who now come to himselfe yet would not rize,
> But still did lie as dead, and quake, and quiver, . . .
>
> EDMUND SPENSER

> To snatch the posy from her swelling breast,
> And loose the ribbon round her slender waist, . . .
>
> JOHN CLARE

We should, however, remember that sometimes pronunciation has changed; when Pope wrote:

> And praise the easy vigour of a line
> Where Denham's strength, and Waller's sweetness, join.

join was pronounced 'jine'; experts on phonetic history are rare, and others must be slow to dogmatize about imperfect rhymes.

An important modern development has been the acceptance of various kinds of imperfect rhyme, to release poets from the restrictions of rhymes that have become hackneyed. Wilfred Owen used what his editor Edmund Blunden called *pararhymes*; they may also be called *consonances, half-rhymes* or *slant rhymes*. Owen was anything but lazy or careless; his consonances are woven into patterns as accurately and formally as the full rhymes of older poets, and he uses full rhymes with confidence. Here is the beginning of his fine poem, *Strange Meeting*:

> It seemed that out of battle I escaped,
> Down some profound dull tunnel, long since scooped
> Through granites which titanic wars had groined.
> Yet also there encumbered sleepers groaned,
> Too fast in thought or death to be bestirred.
> Then, as I probed them, one sprang up and stared
> With pitiless recognition in fixed eyes,
> Lifting distressful hands as if to bless.
> And by his smile, I knew that sullen hall,
> By his dead smile I knew we stood in Hell.

Generally, Wilfred Owen keeps an exact parallel in the consonants, and changes only the vowel sounds, but there are a few exceptions to this:

> Since we believe not otherwise can kind fires burn
> Nor ever suns smile on child, or field, or *fruit*.
> For God's invincible spring our love is made *afraid*;
> Therefore, not loath, we lie out there; therefore we were
> born,
> For love of God seems dying.

Many poets of the present day use consonances like Owen's. Auden, for example, uses them a great deal. Consonances are perhaps appropriate to the present, as they give an impression of rather less certainty than full rhymes, and the present age is, as Auden named it, the Age of Anxiety, full of frightening uncertainties. Here is an example of consonances from Auden; it will be noticed that the first rhyme in the verse is a full rhyme:

> Wrapped in a yielding air, beside
> The flower's soundless hunger,
> Close to the tree's clandestine tide,
> Close to the bird's high fever,
> Loud in his hope and anger,
> Erect about his skeleton,
> Stands the expressive lover,
> Stands the deliberate man.

Assonance, also used by many twentieth-century poets, is the rhyming of vowel sounds without regard for the consonants, as in Louis MacNeice's:

> Not the twilight of the gods but a precise dawn
> Of sallow and grey bricks, and the newsboys crying war.

It is also possible to have an *Unaccented Rhyme*, in which one of the rhyme-syllables is a stressed syllable but the other is not, as in Robert Penn Warren's *Original Sin*:

> But it has not died, it comes, its hand childish, unsure,
> Clutching the bribe of chocolate or a toy you used to
> treasure.

or in George Fraser's *Two Sonnets*:

> The intricacy of the exposed intestines
> Present no easy formal inspiration
> Till art disguises them as wreathing vines.

(It is evident from the two poems from which these lines are taken that the unaccented rhymes are intended to serve as rhymes.)

Apocopated Rhyme occurs when an extra syllable follows only one of the rhyming syllables:

> A poem should be wordless
> As a flight of birds
>
> ARCHIBALD MACLEISH

It is also possible to have a *Light Rhyme* or *Unaccented Rhyme*. *Broken Rhyme*, in which a word is split across the end of the line, is rare but not impossible:

> Leaving him to buy his box of oint-
> Ment, tea and seedlings—which were now the point.
>
> CHRISTOPHER PILLING

and only G. M. Hopkins could risk, in passionately serious poetry:

> But what black Boreas *wrecked her? he*
> Came equipped, deadly *electric* . . .

A *Synthetic Rhyme* is one that asks for some distortion of natural stress or pronunciation; this is fairly common in comic verse:

> We're smart and sober men,
> And quite devoid of fe-ar,
> In all the Royal N.
> None are so smart as we are.
>
> W. S. GILBERT

Serious poetry could hardly go as far as this, but may sometimes claim a licence less grotesque but in principle as daring:

> Some time to have scented change in this procedure,
> our walks to have grown less dank, but richly shadier . . .
>
> KATHLEEN NOTT

This is not confined to the present century:

> Till that he found a little door,
> And therein slipp'd the *key*;
> And there he found three chests in fere
> Of the red and the white mon*ie*.
>
> *The Heir of Linne* (an old ballad)

Mosaic Rhyme, liked by Byron and Browning among others, uses more than one word for at least one of the rhymes:

> So he gowned him,
> Straight got by heart that book to its last page:
> Learned, we found him!
>
> BROWNING

> That hour, o'night's black arch the key-stane,
> That dreary hour he mounts his beast in;
>
> BURNS

There are many other possibilities; for instance, Seamus Heaney in his fine poem *The Salmon Fisher to the Salmon* rhymes: *flail-sea-pull-gravity; casting-reflects-flicking-fleck; perfumed-berries-come-eyes; me-leg-choreography-drag; kill-fly-steel-scaly*; and it works splendidly; or Peter Levi in his wonderful *Christmas Sermon* can risk *desert-hurt, on and on-religion, soul-fall-Bristol.*

Any variant on 'perfect' rhyme can still make patterns that give delight.

VI PHONETIC FORM

(B) ONOMATOPOEIA

> With a quack, quack, here, and a quack, quack, there,
> Here a quack, there a quack, everywhere a quack, quack . . .
>
> *Old MacDonald*

Rhythm obviously helps a great deal in supporting the meaning of the words of a poem; but sometimes the sound of the words also gives great support to the sense. *Cool moonlight*, with long vowels and two l-sounds, certainly sounds more restful and still than *fidgetty kittens*, with short vowels and brittle t-sounds. This tendency in words to echo the meaning by the actual sound is called ONOMATOPOEIA.[1] It is found in an almost pure form in many of the words describing sounds, such as *buzz, fizz, crash, bang, thump, miaow, quack, giggle, sizzle, hiss, sneeze, thud, snort*, and even a long word such as *effervescence*. Sometimes we lose the onomatopoeic effect of words because we do not trouble to pronounce them properly; failing to open our mouths and move our lips and tongues as freely as we should, we turn a vigorous, expressive word into a dull and slovenly sound something like it. To hear a reciter of the calibre of Edith Evans, Laurence Olivier, Carleton Hobbs, or to hear Dylan

[1] The correct adjective is *onomatopoeic* or *onomatopoeical*.

Thomas, T. S. Eliot or Kingsley Amis reciting their own poems, is to find a new intensity in the pleasure of poetry.

The marvellous subtlety of the English language, let alone the supreme subtlety of poetry, is often lost in careless speech.

Onomatopoeia is very common in poetry, but it is difficult to know whether a poet is using it as a deliberate artistic effect or by accident, for so many English words are onomatopoeic that, if the poet chooses the right word in meaning, he is likely automatically to choose the onomatopoeic word. Blake, for example, who took relatively little trouble over technicalities, has such lines as:

> For the gentle wind does move
> Silently, invisibly. . . .

which sounds very quiet with its many l-sounds, f's and v's. And what could sound more bubbly and stream-like than his:

> But a Pebble of the brook
> Warbled out these metres meet

with its b's and r's? The answer to my question is Tennyson's *Brook*, for Tennyson, the more conscious artist and a master of onomatopoeia, gave his brook more of the b's and r's as well as some fluid-sounding l's:

> I chatter over stony ways
> In little sharps and trebles,
> I bubble into eddying bays,
> I babble on the pebbles.

It is not necessary to read this with any exaggeration in order to hear the brook doing all that it says it does. Here are a few more examples from Tennyson:

Slowness and peace suggested by the use of long vowels, l's, m's and n's:

> The long day wanes; the slow moon climbs; the deep
> Moans round with many voices.
>
> *Ulysses*

Three familiar country sounds:

> The sparrow's chirrup on the roof,
> The slow clock ticking, and the sound
> Which to the wooing wind aloof
> The poplar made. . . .
>
> *Mariana*

Peacefulness suggested by l's and many long vowels:

> Music that gentlier on the spirit lies
> Than tired eyelids upon tired eyes;
> Music that brings sweet sleep down from the blissful skies.
> Here are cool mosses deep,
> And through the moss the ivies creep,
> And in the streams the long-leaved flowers weep,
> And from the craggy ledge the poppy hangs in sleep.
>
> *The Lotos-Eaters*

Violence and splintering suggested by hard consonants and short vowels:

> Scarce had she ceased, when out of heaven a bolt
> (For now the storm was close above them) struck,
> Furrowing a giant oak, and javelining

With darted spikes and splinters of the wood
The dark earth round.

Merlin and Vivien

Presently, too, Vivien in the thunderstorm is

dazzled by the livid-flickering forks,
And deafened by the stammering cracks and claps.

Violence is again to be found in:

last a heathen horde,
Reddening the sun with smoke and earth with blood,
And on the spike that split the mother's heart
Spitting the child. . . .

The Coming of Arthur

Pope was another poet with a great conscious awareness of the use of onomatopoeia. He refers to it as a very necessary part of a poet's technique:

'Tis not enough no harshness gives offence,
The sound must seem an echo to the sense.
Soft is the strain when Zephyr gently blows,
And the smooth stream in smoother numbers flows;
But when loud surges lash the sounding shore,
The hoarse, rough verse should like the torrent roar.
When Ajax strives, some rock's vast weight to throw,
The line too labours, and the words move slow;
Not so, when swift Camilla scours the plain,
Flies o'er the unbending corn, and skims along the main.

An Essay on Criticism

Notably skilled users of onomatopoeia in the present century include T. S. Eliot, Edith Sitwell, Dylan Thomas,

Edwin Morgan, George Macbeth, Sylvia Plath. Poems containing many onomatopoeic effects are particularly suitable for reading aloud and for choral speaking. Onomatopoeia may attract us not only by the accuracy with which it gives a sound-picture of the things or events it describes, but also by lulling us into a trance as a kind of incantation. Vachel Lindsay has specialized in this aspect of onomatopoeia in such poems as *The Congo, The Santa Fé Trail* and *The Ghosts of the Buffaloes*. Some of Edith Sitwell's earliest poems are little more than wonderful patterns of sound such as have probably never been surpassed in their kind; the student will enjoy reading her *Trio for Two Cats and a Trombone, Three Poor Witches, The Wind's Bastinado, Country Dance, Hornpipe* and *Sir Beelzebub*. The reader who is seriously interested in the study of how particular speech sounds have particular mental effects can probably study nothing more helpful than Edith Sitwell's *A Poet's Notebook* and her *Alexander Pope*.

It seems probable that at this stage in the history of our literature when criticism has come of age and almost every possible aspect of poetry has been analysed in minute detail —far more detail than is anywhere possible in this little book—poets are using sound effects and other technical devices more consciously than ever before. This is not invariably a good thing; great art is more than technical virtuosity, and a self-conscious writing for analytical critics may sometimes tempt to insincerities. However, we cannot repudiate any knowledge we gain, and it will be interesting to see the further developments of poetry in this wonderfully fruitful and experimental era. It is extremely unlikely that many poets, having learned some facts about onomatopoeic effects from studying other poems, apply them with a formulated technique; the result would probably sound dull and laboured. The fact that the most suitable word is often also the onomatopoeically effective word depends on aspects of language so primitive that we are seldom conscious of them while we are using the words.

The student may like to read a few general hints on the effect of some speech sounds used onomatopoeically. These should not be taken as a statement of fact; the effect will depend very much on the context and the other sounds found in juxtaposition.

In general, long vowels tend to sound more peaceful or more solemn than short ones, which tend to give an impression of quick movement, agitation or triviality.

b *and* p	explosive sounds, suggest quickness, movement, triviality, scorn.
m, n, ng	provide various effects of humming, singing, music, occasionally sinister.
l	suggests liquids in motion, streams, water, rest, peace, luxury, voluptuousness.
k, g, st, ts, ch, qu	suggest harshness, violence, cruelty, movement, discomfort, noise, conflict.
s, sh	hissing, also soft and smooth, soothing sounds. Robert Graves points out[1] that the correct manipulation of the letter S is important to a poet, for too many S's are over-conspicuous in a line.

[1] In *On English Poetry*.

	At all times a bad reader who prolongs s-sounds can spoil a poem.
z	tends to appear in contexts of harshness.
f, w	and to a lesser extent v, suggest wind, wings and any motion of a light and easy kind.
t, d	are like k, g, but less emphatic, and are much used in contexts where short actions are described.
r	more perhaps than the other sounds, depends on the sounds near it, but is generally found in contexts of movement and noise.
th (hard or soft)	tends to be quiet and soothing.

Often a predominance of vowels tends to suggest something slow, peaceful, pleasant, while a general clatter of crowded consonants suggests greater speed, excitement or harshness.

VII PHONETIC FORM

(C) INTERNAL PATTERN

Whereat with blade, with bloody blameful blade,
He bravely broached his boiling bloody breast.
SHAKESPEARE: *A Midsummer Night's Dream*

Symmetry of form in a poem is achieved chiefly by the rhythm-pattern and the rhyme-scheme, but, just as a fine painting has a magnificent total form and yet it is possible for a book on art to print a reproduction of a 'detail', one face or foot or tree, to show the skill of the artist, so a poem can have details within the main structure. These details include alliteration, all kinds of internal rhymes, assonances, echoes and various kinds of repetition and contrast. Many of these devices have long Greek names that no one uses nowadays and that make no difference to our enjoyment or admiration. An amusing example of the over-pedantic approach may be found in the 'Glosse' (notes) to Spenser's *The Shepheards Calender*, in which Spenser's friend E.K. comments on the lines

I love thilke lasse, (alas! why doe I love?)
And am forlorne, (alas! why am I lorne?)

thus: 'A pretty Epanorthosis in these two verses; and withal a Paranomasia or playing with the word. . . .' We can enjoy the trivial prettiness of the trick without this help.

However, to have an ear for these internal patterns is to enjoy poetry more. Alliteration, one of the most generally used internal ornaments, was once the very basis of the physical form of English poetry. Anglo-Saxon poetry, the earliest English literature, includes poems written in alliterative verse, such as *Beowulf, The Dream of the Rood* and *The Battle of Maldon*, magnificent works of art which, for their merit, deserve to be much better known, but will probably never be well known even to the British, since Anglo-Saxon is quite a difficult language to learn and is of less practical use than Latin, Greek or Sanskrit, being a dead language without a continuing tradition.[1] To sum up the rules of Anglo-Saxon poetry in a very hasty manner, three words in each line had to begin with the same letter; there were patterns of rhythm obeying fairly strict rules, but no rhymes. The composers of these poems seem to have been highly conscious artists, for there are a number of allusions to the bard's 'word-hoard' and the need to 'wrestle with words'. This method of alliteration, known as 'head-rhyme', continued to be practised as late as the end of the fourteenth century with William Langland's poem *The Vision of Piers Plowman*. However, as soon as English poets had learned the method of rhyme from continental poets, alliteration be-

[1] Anglo-Saxon or Old English is the language used in England before 1066, and cannot be understood without learning it as a separate language. Middle English is the language used roughly 1066–1500 and can be understood with occasional reference to a glossary. All the best works of Anglo-Saxon literature have now been translated, *Beowulf* at least fifty-six times into various languages. Gavin Bone's *Anglo-Saxon Poetry*, OUP, 1943, is a pleasant introduction. Details of the available translations may be found in *The New Cambridge Bibliography of English Literature*, vol. I, cols 245–6.

came less important, sinking from being the essential feature of poetic structure to being a decoration. This must have made poetry more flexible, since it is easier to find one appropriate rhyme per line than to work out a series of lines each with three alliterating words.

Alliteration is near to being an instinctive method of emphasis; in Shaw's *Pygmalion* the phonetic expert Henry Higgins is rebuked by his housekeeper for applying a certain vulgar word to 'your boots, to the butter and to the brown bread', and excuses himself by saying: 'Oh! that! Mere alliteration, Mrs Pearce, natural to a poet.' If we observe our own conversation, we may notice many alliterations. Many proverbial and idiomatic expressions gain much of their force from alliteration, for example: 'Fine feathers make fine birds'; 'All is not gold that glitters'; 'Speech is silvern, silence is golden'. We speak of something being in 'bits and bobs' or decked in 'buttons and bows'; we strive with 'might and main' to find something of which we have not lately seen 'hide or hair' and candidates at elections talk of 'peace and prosperity' rather than 'peace and wealth'.

Since alliteration plays such a part in common speech, it is probable that not all alliteration in poetry is deliberate; as with onomatopoeia, the words that are intellectually right tend also to be the words that are most attractive in sound. Christopher Smart was of doubtful sanity when he wrote *A Song to David*, with such charming alliterations as:

> *S*weet is the lily's *s*ilver bell,
> And *s*weet the *w*akeful tapers' *s*mell
> That *w*atch for early prayer.
>
> *W*alk, *w*ater, meditated *w*ild,
> And all the *b*loomy *b*eds.

Precious the *r*uby's *bl*ushing *bl*aze
And alba's *bl*est imperial *r*ays,

Blake, too, produced probably without conscious intent, effects like this:

*S*weet *s*leep, with *s*oft down, . . .

*B*ring me my *b*ow of *b*urning gold!

*W*eeping in *w*eak and mortal clay. . . .

When we turn to the more deliberately literary poets, we find a great deal of alliteration, often in very elaborate patterns, so that poetry almost becomes embroidery. There are no technical terms at present in general use for the different kinds of alliteration, but two types with rather different effects can be distinguished: one I will call *piled alliteration*, in which the initial letter is repeated several times to give a cumulative effect, and which is generally used for emphasis; the other has been called *crossed alliteration*, in which two or more initial letters are woven into a pattern, perhaps in alternation, to give a kind of balance. The second is by far the more subtle kind and probably the more attractive.

Piled alliteration for emphasis is to be found in facetious contexts, as in the motto to this chapter, and also in serious contexts, as:

Into this Universe, and *Wh*y not knowing,
Nor *Wh*ence, like *W*ater, *w*illy-nilly flowing,
And out of it, as *W*ind along the *W*aste,
I know not *W*hither, *w*illy-nilly blowing.

FITZGERALD: *Rubáiyát of Omar Khayyám*

And all should cry, *B*eware! *B*eware!
His *fl*ashing eyes, his *fl*oating hair!
COLERIDGE: *Kubla Khan*

All the *b*lue *b*onnets are *b*ound for the *B*order.
SCOTT

Push off, and *s*itting well in order *s*mite
The *s*ounding furrows; for my purpose holds
To *s*ail beyond the *s*unset. . . .
TENNYSON: *Ulysses*

Or bid me *d*ie, and I will *d*are
E'en *d*eath to *d*ie for thee.
HERRICK: *To Anthea, who may command him anything*

Here are some examples of the more subtle effect of crossed alliteration:

No *l*onger *m*ourn for *m*e when I am dead
Than you shall hear the *s*urly *s*ullen bell
Give *w*arning to the *w*orld that I am fled
From this *v*ile *w*orld, w*i*th *v*ilest *w*orms to dwell:
Nay, if you *r*ead this *l*ine, *r*emember not
The hand that *wr*it it; for I *l*ove you so
That I in your sweet *th*oughts would be forgot
If *th*inking on me then should make you woe.[1]
SHAKESPEARE

In these lines it will be noticed that where there is strong, direct emphasis, as in the 'surly sullen bell', there is piled alliteration, but the pattern of alliteration becomes more complex as the thought becomes more subtle.

[1] *Wr*, of course, alliterates to *r*, and *th*inking does not alliterate with *th*en; we must always be guided by the ear, not the eye.

How *s*oon hath *T*ime, the *s*ubtle *th*ief of *y*outh,
*S*tol'n on his wing my *th*ree and *t*wentieth *y*ear!
MILTON

has crossed alliteration on four different consonants. Here are a few more examples:

Time and *d*eath shall *d*epart and say in *f*lying
*L*ove has *f*ound out a way to *l*ive by *d*ying.
DRYDEN

Come *Sl*eep; O *Sl*eep! the *c*ertain knot of *p*eace,
The *b*aiting-*p*lace of *w*it, the *b*alm of *w*oe,
The *p*oor man's *w*ealth, the *p*risoner's release. . . .
SIR PHILIP SIDNEY

*F*air eyes, who asks more *h*eat than comes from *h*ence,
He in a *f*ever wishes pestilence.
DONNE

Give *l*ife to this *d*ark *w*orld *w*hich *l*ieth *d*ead.
DRUMMOND OF HAWTHORNDEN

While the Cock with lively *d*in
*S*catters the rear of *d*arkness thin
And to the *st*ack, or the *B*arn *d*ore,
*St*outly *st*ruts his *D*ames *b*efore.
MILTON: *L'Allegro*

Alliteration is by no means the only kind of repeated sound in a poem other than rhyme.[1] Let us look at a verse from John Donne:

[1] Though in common usage *alliteration* refers only to initial letters or letter combinations, some critics include other repetitions of sounds under that name.

> *Wh*en *th*ou *s*igh'st, *th*ou *s*igh'st not *w*ind
> But *s*igh'st my *s*oul away;
> *Wh*en thou *w*eep'st, unkindly kind,
> My life's blood *d*oth *d*ecay.
> It cannot be,
> *Th*at *th*ou *l*ov'st me, as *th*ou say'st,
> If in *th*ine my *l*ife *th*ou *w*aste,
> *Th*at art the best of me.

First of all, there is an obvious pattern of alliteration; but there is also a frequent repetition of the i-sound in 'sigh', 'kindly', 'thine', 'my', 'life' and (then) 'wind'. This is a sound whose common emotional significance can be guessed from its appearance in such words as 'whining', 'pining', 'crying', 'sighing', 'decline'—a sound often suggesting sorrow and depression.[1] It is also a rather long vowel which slows the movement of the lines in their naturally rather rapid rhythm. The numerous -st sounds are dictated by grammatical necessity rather than art, but the repetition does help to build up emphasis, and contributes something to the effect of the s-alliteration.

In Milton's beautiful word-picture:

> . . . the high embowed roof,
> With antic pillars massy proof,
> And storied windows richly dight,
> Casting a dim religious light.
> There let the pealing organ blow
> To the full-voiced choir below,

alliteration, though it exists, is not dominant. There are

[1] I am well aware that the vowel is also found in *dining* and *wining*; it is dangerous to generalize too *wildly*.

several other kinds of sound-echo. As a bit of red ribbon at the throat of a dress may be 'caught up' by a red bracelet on the wrist, so 'pillars' and 'windows' catch up each other's sounds, and 'storied' and 'organ' do so even more, being words with the same stressed vowel followed by an unstressed vowel which has become neutral in its unstressed position. Re*lig*ious has in the centre a link between the vowel of *dim* and the initial consonant of *light*, and 'light' and 'let' (in the next line) are perfect pararhymes. The l-sound keeps appearing in the middle of words. There are several other internal echoes that I am deliberately leaving for the intelligent reader to find.

Perhaps in *The Raven* Edgar Allen Poe rather overdoes the use of internal rhymes, alliterations, echoes and resemblances of all kinds; but it will be instructive and perhaps interesting for the reader to work out all these in the final verse:

And the Raven, never flitting, still is sitting, still is sitting
On the pallid bust of Pallas, just above my chamber door;
And his eyes have all the seeming of a demon's that is
    dreaming,
And the lamplight o'er him streaming throws his shadow
    on the floor
And my soul from out that shadow that lies floating on the
    floor
Shall be lifted—nevermore!

Swinburne is another poet who uses a great many internal echoes:

And the high gods took in hand
Fire, and the falling of tears,

And a measure of sliding sand
From under the feet of the years;
And froth and drift of the sea;
And dust of the labouring earth;
And bodies of things to be
In the houses of death and birth;
And wrought with weeping and laughter,
And fashioned with loathing and love
With life before and after
And death beneath and above,
For a day and a night and a morrow,
That his strength might endure for a span
With travail and heavy sorrow,
The holy spirit of man.

Sometimes Swinburne uses this technique to excess, but he was witty enough to parody himself in *Nephelidia*:

From the depth of the dreamy decline of the dawn through
a notable nimbus of nebulous moonshine,
Pallid and pink as the palm of the flag-flower that flickers
with fear of the flies as they float,
Are the looks of our lovers that lustrously lean from a
marvel of mystic miraculous moonshine,
These that we feel in the blood of our blushes that thicken
and threaten with throbs through the throat? . . .

VIII FORM IN INTONATION

'. . . so I had to put my foot down in a very firm tone of voice . . .'
Heard in a school staff-room

It is possible for a poem to have quite a definite pattern of intonation, a pattern made only when the poem is read aloud, by the changes of pitch and stress. This pattern is more at the mercy of the reader than any other, for, as is well known, we can alter the meaning of a sentence entirely by altering the intonation. A friend of mine tells me that she knows a highly intelligent woman who is so completely tone-deaf as not to understand when a sentence is spoken ironically; she has several times been much embarrassed as a result. If we misunderstand the meaning of a poem we are likely to read it with the wrong intonation, much as, in *A Midsummer Night's Dream*, Peter Quince, reciting mechanically a Prologue he does not understand, runs over all the stops and talks nonsense:

> Consider then we come but in despite.
> We do not come as minding to content you.
> Our true intent is. All for your delight
> We are not here. That you should here repent you,
> The actors are at hand. . . .

Poems in which the intonation-pattern is important for making a pattern of sound as well as conveying the sense will tend to be those written in an ironical temper and in a colloquial style. There is an exact parallel of intonation in these two verses by Sir John Suckling:

> Why so pale and wan, fond lover?
> Prithee, why so pale?
> Will, when looking well can't win her,
> Looking ill prevail?
> Prithee, why so pale?
>
> Why so dull and mute, young sinner?
> Prithee, why so mute?
> Will, when speaking well can't win her,
> Saying nothing do't?
> Prithee, why so mute?

This repetition leads us, as with a pattern of rhythm, to expect a third repetition of the pattern, and we receive an agreeable, amusing shock when the last verse has a very different intonation:

> Quit, quit for shame, this will not move;
> This cannot take her.
> If of herself she will not love,
> Nothing can make her;
> The devil take her!

The half-sympathetic, reasoning tone of the first two verses gives place to a robust and hearty dismissal of the whole matter.

Abraham Cowley, in his light-hearted poem *The Chronicle*, in which he relates a succession of love-fancies with great good humour, repeats a pattern of intonation in the middle of the poem, where he twice refers to one lady's conquest, moves in the fourth line into an explanation of how this queen was deposed and in the final line discloses the name of the new fancy:

> Another Mary then arose
> And did the rigorous laws impose;
> A mighty tyrant she!
> Long, alas, should I have been
> Under that iron-sceptred queen,
> Had not Rebecca set me free.
>
> When fair Rebecca set me free,
> 'Twas then a golden time with me.
> But soon these pleasures fled,
> For the gracious princess died
> In her youth and beauty's pride,
> And Judith reigned in her stead.

To read the whole of the poem is to see how, though he is relating a catalogue, Cowley skilfully shifts the intonation patterns so that no pattern becomes stereotyped, which would make a poem of such length very dull.

There is a very close parallel of intonation in the last two verses of Burns's *To the Unco Guid*; the parallel emphasizes the move away from severe satire to gentle regret and charity; to use one verse only would perhaps have made the poem seem 'top-heavy' or inconsistent in tone:

> Then gently scan your brother man,
> Still gentler sister woman;
> Thou they may gang a kennin wrang,
> To step aside is human;

One point must still be greatly dark—
The moving *Why* they do it;
And just as lamely can ye mark
How far perhaps they rue it.

Who made the heart, 'tis He alone
Decidedly can try us;
He knows each chord, its various tone,
Each spring, its various bias;
Then at the balance let's be mute;
We never can adjust it;
What's done we partly may compute,
But know not what's resisted.

Edmund Waller's *On A Girdle* has in each verse two lines of statement followed by two more strongly emotional lines; the intonation for the three verses is probably much the same, with a somewhat louder voice for the last two lines:

That which her slender waist confined,
Shall now my joyful temples bind;
No monarch but would give his crown,
His arms might do what this has done.

It was my heaven's extremest sphere,
The pale which held that lovely deer.
My joy, my grief, my hope, my love,
Did all within this circle move!

A narrow compass! and yet there
Dwelt all that's good and all that's fair;
Give me but what this ribband bound,
Take all the rest the sun goes round.

Here, of course, the intonation is far from exactly symmetrical.

While it is interesting to look for parallels and patterns of intonation in a poem, it is more generally instructive to notice how wonderfully a great poet will avoid monotony, and how a good reciter follows the intention of the poet.

IX THE USE OF REPETITION

(A) INTELLECTUAL EFFECT

A double blessing is a double grace.
SHAKESPEARE: *Hamlet*

Whenever we start discussing pattern in poetry, we are discussing repetition; rhythm, rhyme, alliteration and internal echoes are all repetitions of sounds; but the repetition of whole words or phrases is part of both intellectual and physical form. We all know how repetition helps us to learn such things as the conjugation of a foreign verb or a list of dates, and how much advertising and propaganda depend on repetition to convince us of things that are often not true. All teachers soon find that they have to say something several times before every member of the class has absorbed it. We also tend to repeat ourselves when we are very angry, happy, or distressed, and those who have never acquired the art of conversation irritate us by repeating themselves far too much. The repetition of words is used for emphasis in all these situations. The repetition of a word or a phrase for the sake of this intellectual effect—to emphasize a fact or idea—is quite different from the function of repetition in a refrain or chorus; this will be treated in the next chapter.

Repetition of a single word is very common, as in speech;

it is used for emphasis, much as an Indian friend of mine used to describe a kitten as a 'small small cat'.

A little buttery, and therein
A little bin
Which keeps my little loaf of bread
Unchipp'd, unflead:

HERRICK

The mountains look on Marathon
And Marathon looks on the sea.

BYRON

It is the cause, it is the cause, my soul!
Let me not name it to you, you chaste stars!
It is the cause.

SHAKESPEARE

Sleep, O sleep,
With thy rod of incantation,
Charm my imagination.

GAY

Fallen, fallen, fallen, fallen, fallen from his high estate.

DRYDEN

A single word may also be repeated many times in order to work up to an emotional climax:

Let him have time to tear his curled hair,
Let him have time against himself to rave,
Let him have time of Time's help to despair,
Let him have time to live a loathed slave,
Let him have time a beggar's orts to crave,
And time to see one that by alms doth live
Disdain to him disdained scraps to give.

Let him have time to see his friends his foes,
And merry fools to mock at him resort;
Let him have time to mark how slow time goes
In time of sorrow, and how swift and short
His time of folly, and his time of sport;
And ever let his unrecalling crime
Have time to wail the abusing of his time.

SHAKESPEARE: *The Rape of Lucrece*

How do I love thee? Let me count the ways.
I love thee to the depth and breadth and height
My soul can reach, when feeling out of sight
For the ends of Being and ideal Grace.
I love thee to the level of everyday's
Most quiet need, by sun and candlelight.
I love thee freely, as men strive for Right;
I love thee purely, as they turn from Praise.
I love thee with the passion put to use
In my own griefs, and with my childhood's faith.
I love thee with a love I seemed to lose
With my lost saints,—I love thee with the breath,
Smiles, tears, of all my life!—and, if God choose,
I shall but love thee better after death.

ELIZABETH BARRETT BROWNING

In the hands of a master this prolonged repetition can be thus magnificent. Obviously, in an inferior poet, who resembles not so much the brilliant artist as the bad talker, it can be very dull. The

Ay me, alas! ay me, alas! come, Time, take everything
away,
For all is thine, be it good or bad that grows.

of the minor Elizabethan poet Thomas Proctor is not particularly impressive, nor is Tennyson's *Riflemen Form*; all readers of poetry should bear in mind that, just as there are many fine poems written by minor poets, sometimes single poems by which alone a poet is known, there are many lapses in the work of most of the major poets. We should never be completely and slavishly uncritical.

The repetition of a phrase is as common as the repetition of a word, and, like the repetition of a word, serves to give emphasis:

> If arts and schools reply,
> Give arts and schools the lie.
>
> SIR WALTER RALEIGH

> Dost thou laugh to see how fools are vexed
> To add to golden numbers, golden numbers?
>
> DEKKER

> In vain, in vain—the all-composing hour
> Resistless falls: the Muse obeys the Power.
> She comes! she comes! the sable throne behold
> Of Night primeval and of Chaos old!
>
> POPE: *The Dunciad*

> All we are against thee, against thee, O God most high.
>
> SWINBURNE

> I am! yet what I am who cares, or knows?
>
> JOHN CLARE

> Arm! Arm! it is—it is—the cannon's opening roar!
>
> BYRON: *Childe Harold's Pilgrimage*

I fear a Man of frugal Speech—
I fear a Silent Man—

EMILY DICKINSON

Repetition, not of an exact phrase but of the structure of a phrase, is a very common device:

Like the dew on the mountain,
Like the foam on the river,
Like the bubble on the fountain,
Thou art gone, and for ever!

SCOTT

My heart is like a singing bird
Whose nest is in a watered shoot;
My heart is like an apple tree
Whose boughs are bent with thickset fruit;

CHRISTINA ROSSETTI

For one good wife Ulysses slew
A worthy knot of gentle blood;
For one ill wife Greece overthrew
The town of Troy. Sith bad and good
Bring mischief, Lord, let be Thy will
To keep me free from either ill.

ANONYMOUS (sixteenth century)

Where you were wont to have caudles for your head,
Now must you munch mammocks and lumps of bread;
And where you had changes of rich array,
Now lap you in a coverlet full fain that ye may;
And where that ye were pomped with what ye wold,
Now must ye suffer both hunger and cold.

JOHN SKELTON

The Samurai find time enough to pause,
Touch the enchanted handles of their swords
And finger the dulling metal of their blades.

JAMES FENTON

There are other and considerably more subtle devices of repetition. It is possible to play with a word, using it several times with a slightly different meaning each time:

Diaphenia, like the spreading roses,
That in thy sweet all sweets encloses,
Fair sweet, how I do love thee!
I do love thee as each flower
Loves the sun's life-giving power;
For dead, thy breath to life might move me.

HENRY CONSTABLE

This is pretty but trivial; but how shatteringly startling, how daring, in the best sense, is the passionate and holy pun at the end of John Donne's *Hymn to God the Father*:[1]

I have a sin of fear, that when I have spun
My last thread, I shall perish on the shore;
Swear by Thyself that at my death Thy Son
Shall shine as he shines now and heretofore;
And having done that Thou hast done,
I fear no more.

The 'Son' is a 'sun' that shines as well as the Son of God; the final repetition of 'done' makes a symmetrical pattern with the other two verses of this lovely poem, but I feel sure that the poet is also saying 'Thou, God, hast Donne—in Thy

[1] We know that the name Donne was pronounced to rhyme with *bun*.

keeping for ever'. Puns can evidently be sublime as well as vulgar.[1]

It is possible to repeat something with a slight change to improve the modulation:

> For the sword outwears the sheath,
> And the soul wears out the breast.
>
> BYRON

Or, when ideas are paralleled, the number of words used for each idea, or the number of syllables, may be varied so as to avoid monotony in the rhythm:

> The One remains, the many change and pass;
> Heaven's light for ever shines, Earth's shadows fly.
>
> SHELLEY: *Adonais*

> For he who lives more lives than one
> More deaths than one must die.
>
> OSCAR WILDE

Some slight reversal or modification of the normal word order may lend great weight to the words:

> Some little talk awhile of Me and Thee
> There was—and then no more of Thee and Me.
>
> *Rubáiyát of Omar Khayyám*

> Hierusalem, my happy home,
> When shall I come to thee?
> When shall my sorrows have an end?
> Thy joys when shall I see?
>
> ANONYMOUS (seventeenth century)

[1] See also Chapter XIII.

This kind of device needs to be used with discretion, or the poet will invert the word order so artificially that the result is unpleasant. Inversion is supposed to be a feature of 'poetic licence' and is freely used by beginners and bad poets who cannot otherwise push their rhyme words to the end of the lines, but good poets use it only (in their good poems) where it also gives some special emphasis. This is from a noble and very popular poem, but is it not somewhat dislocated?

> Oft did the harvest to their sickle yield,
> Their furrow oft the stubborn glebe has broke;
> How jocund did they drive their team afield!
> How bowed the woods beneath their sturdy stroke!
>
> GRAY: *Elegy Written in A Country Churchyard*

It is plain that here Gray is trying to repeat a general idea in four examples without monotony, but he has altered the word order so much as to upset the natural flow of the English language. He was writing in a period of much artificiality; but it may also be helpful to remember that Gray, like many of the most artificial of English poets, had a classical education, and was accustomed to the literatures of Latin and Greek, in which word-order obeys different rules and has more to do with emphasis.

Another type of repetition for its intellectual effect is the repetition of the whole structure of a verse, with only a few words changed; to demonstrate this I must quote a whole poem:

O she looked out of the window,
As white as any milk;
But he looked into the window
As black as any silk.

Hulloa, hulloa, hulloa, hulloa you coal black smith!
O what is your silly song?
You never shall change my maiden name
That I have kept so long;

I'd rather die a maid, yes, but then she said,
And be buried all in my grave,
Than I'd have such a nasty, husky, dusky, musty, fusky
 coal black smith;
A maiden I will die.

Then she became a duck,
A duck upon the stream;
And he became a water-dog,
And fetched her back again.
Hulloa, etc.

Then she became a hare,
A hare all on the plain;
And he became a greyhound dog
And fetched her back again.
Hulloa, etc.

Then she became a fly,
A fly all in the air;
And he became a spider,
And fetched her to his lair.
Hulloa, etc.[1]

This form in which the main structure remains the same is a favourite of folk-song and other traditional songs that have

[1] There are several versions of this song and many more of the general story. I am indebted for this version to Auden and Garrett: *The Poet's Tongue.*

developed in communities and been composed by groups rather than individuals. I do not doubt that practically every residential college, school or barracks in the country still composes such songs. Because repetition generally reinforces some idea, repetition can also be used for ironical effect; the reader is lulled into an expectation, then shocked by some unexpected twist. Robert Graves in the poem *Call it a Good Marriage* tells us several times to do just that, but brings us to the conclusion:

> Till as jurymen we sat upon
> Two deaths by suicide.

A. E. Housman in *Is my team ploughing* lets a youth in his grave ask questions of a friend, who gives him genial, reassuring answers: yes, ploughing goes on, football goes on, his former sweetheart is happy once more, his friend is well . . . until we learn in the last verse that the pattern of wistful question and comforting answer is not so simple: the old friend is now living with the old sweetheart.

X THE USE OF REPETITION

(B) PURE MAGICAL EFFECT

Thrice toss these oaken ashes in the air,
Thrice sit thou mute in this enchanted chair,
Then thrice three times tie up this true-love's knot,
And murmur soft, 'She will or she will not'.

THOMAS CAMPION

Magic makes great use of repetitions; in many folk-tales something has to be done or said three or seven times; religious rituals, which are more or less akin to primitive magic, depending on the degree of intellectual development, make great use of repetition with prayers for the various occasions of life, prayer-wheels, rosaries and repeated observances; and repetition plays a great part in the more primitive, emotional parts of our lives. Magic spells, in very diverse cultures all over the world, are almost invariably very repetitive.[1] We are reassured by someone else repeating our own name in a tender and friendly manner, demoralized by someone repeating it in hostile or sarcastic tones. By repeating a word we seem to gain a sense of power over it: many dull talkers repeat what they think is

[1] See Robin Skelton, *Spellcraft*, Routledge & Kegan Paul, London, 1978.

a good phrase; children repeat new words they have learned with a persistence often wearying to adults; and older people often take the first opportunity to use a word they have just learned. The habit of swearing, especially when it becomes a habit divorced from emphasis, may have some such primitive significance; most of the English swear-words have meanings connected with religion, blood, or fertility, three of the very primitive human interests. When we study poetry intellectually, we must think of its effect on us and try to account for it; but we should not forget that if the poem is a good one the poet probably wrote it under the stimulus of some overwhelmingly powerful emotional urge, and some of the poet's emotion may be passed on to us by processes that are not conscious. Poetry is more akin to magic, prayer, prophecy and myth than to knitting or fretwork; to look at it purely from the formally technical point of view and never surrender to it is as misleading as to wallow all the time in indefinable emotion about it.

Poetry has some kinship with the language of religion. Part of the immense pathos and emotional power of religious ritual and liturgy lies precisely in its *lack* of originality. The poignancy of the formulae of a funeral service is that they have been said many times over other bodies, in the presence of other mourners, and are thus loaded with the whole problem of human anguish at the inevitability of death. The marriage service of the Church of England is profoundly moving largely because the terrible vows have been made before so many times, and are, in a sense, quite impossible of fulfilment and represent only the best aspirations of imperfect beings crystallized into a formula; these words are loaded with a million memories of effort and failure, hope and happiness and sorrow. Until the *Alterna-*

tive Service Book was published in 1980, most of the language of these rituals went back to 1552.

An example of the close relationship of ritual and poetry is to be found in the beautiful and terrifying *Lyke-Wake Dirge*. It consists of a summary of what the dead are to expect in their journey towards heaven: Purgatory fire, the Brig' O'Dread, Whinny-muir[1] and the consequences of their own evil actions or the relief brought by their good actions. This is intellectual enough; indeed, in its simple justice it is almost mathematical:

> If ever thou gavest hosen and shoon,
> Sit thee down and put them on;
>
> If hosen and shoon thou ne'er gavest none,
> The whinnies shall prick thee to the bare bone. . . .

but, like a pulse beat under the summary of the facts, runs a double refrain. Let us look at the first verse with its refrain:

> This ae night, this ae night,
> *Every night and all*,
> Fire and fleet and candle-light,
> *And Christ receive thy saule.*

The use of 'Every night and all' adds nothing to the intellectual meaning of the poem; to say it once would theoretically be sufficient; but the repetition heightens the emotional effect of its real, implied meaning, which is something like this: 'This watch by the dead has to take place every night; people die every day; you too must die, perhaps sooner than you think; every night brings its own peril of death.' More important, 'And Christ receive thy saule' is the proper,

[1] Thorny Moor.

traditional thing to say; it is helpful to the fleeting soul, yet by its finality it is also terrifying. (For many years, a British judge sentencing someone to death added 'May the Lord have mercy on your soul'; this must have been similarly both compassionate and, in its inexorable finality, terrifying.) There is the further implication: 'Soon we shall say this formula again—for you.'

Many old ballads have a refrain which appears to be nearly meaningless but carries very heavy implications. There is a well-known ballad, generally called *The Cruel Mother*, telling of a woman who murders her twin babies to save herself from disgrace, and is later haunted by their ghosts and tortured by remorse. This horrible theme has for its double refrain 'Fine flowers in the valley' and 'And the green leaves they grow rarely'. These lines seem almost frivolously pretty in such a context, but in fact they serve to emphasize the grim theme by contrast, as a white background emphasizes a black object. Spring, the time for joyful reckless love, the flower of the valley (not the austere loneliness of the mountain heights), love so often compared to a flower for its beauty or its transience, but also risking the shameful fruit of unwise love; delight in the miracle of Spring that always withers—these are the suggestions; the ballad ends with an additional refrain line which is horrifyingly ironical in its context of eternal torment:

> But now we're in the heavens hie,
> Fine flowers in the valley—
> And ye have the pains of hell to drie,
> And the green leaves they grow rarely.
> Ten thousand times good-night and be wi' thee.

This is rather like the madness of Ophelia, increasing the sense of horror by allusions to pretty things.

Dunbar in his famous *Lament for the Makaris* (poets) uses as his refrain *Timor mortis conturbat me* (The fear of death disturbs me). Latin as an ornament to Scots verse may seem a little incongruous, perhaps even affected; it was not unusual in Dunbar's day, but it is also very impressive by its associations. Latin was the language of Catholic ritual, so the suggestion of a burial service heightens the sense both of fear and of the inevitability of death—the common human situation for which the formulae are provided. There may be a further implication: 'I use a Latin tag, therefore I am an educated man, a "clerk" not a "lewd man", and I can speak authoritatively about the death of poets.'

Not all refrains, however, are so obvious in their function, so indisputably meaningful. *Binnorie*, a favourite ballad, has as its refrains: 'Binnorie, O Binnorie!' and 'By the bonny mill-dams o' Binnorie' which, while appropriate enough to some of the verses, are absurdly inappropriate to others. The ballad of *Earl Brand* has as its refrains the meaningless 'Ay lally, O lilly lally', curiously light and gay for the grim theme, and 'All in the night so early', which is not appropriate to the whole poem. Little sense can be extracted from the refrain 'As the dow (dove) flies over the mulberry tree' in *The Riddling Knight*, 'With a hey lillelu and a how lo lan' and 'And the birk and the broom blows bonnie' in *Hynd Horn*, or 'Eh, wow, bonnie!' in *Babylon*, in which the story is anything but 'bonnie'! The early ballads are the best-known English poems with refrains, though many, including some of the greatest, have none. Some of the early carols, in the wide sense of the word, which does not confine them to Christmas carols,[1] have refrains that sound more like exercises for the correction of faulty speech than poetry. Some of these may have existed mainly to help people to keep time in the dance which was an accompaniment of primitive song. This refrain from a Furry Day Carol:[2]

> With Holan-to, sing merry, O,
> With Holan-to, sing merry,
> With Holan-to, sing merry, O,
> With Holan-to, sing merry!

is to modern ears meaningless to the point of being irritating, though it originally celebrated the *Halantow*, a bunch of flowers carried on a pole in what may be a survival of Druidic ceremony.

The refrain that seems meaningless, or that does not carry the sense or the narrative forward, can be boring or even embarrassing to the self-conscious modern reader, and is extremely difficult to use in recitation, unless it is so onomatopoeic that it can be used frankly as a sound effect, as in *Old MacDonald Had a Farm*, sea shanties with a hauling movement, the railway song *Chickahanka*, or some of Vachel Lindsay. If such refrains have to be spoken they are generally more suitable for choral speech than for individual recitation; most primitive poetry seems to have been collective rather than personal. When the ballads were first recited the audience very likely joined in the chorus, perhaps with

[1] The *Oxford Book of Carols*, OUP, London, 1928, often reprinted, is the most accessible volume to give some idea of the range.

[2] *Furry* Day here means *Flowery* Day—May Day, celebrated in the Cornish Furry Day festivities on 8 May.

some accompaniment such as clapping or stamping.[1] The refrain, in early poetry, may have had a function nowadays better known to most of us in such debased uses as the political slogan, the televised advertising jingle or some kinds of commercialized popular music: repetition brings about a state not far from hypnosis, in which we more readily accept suggestions. In a context of meaningful ritual and honest art, this must often have helped people to manage and enrich their emotions, whereas debased uses merely supplement our natural stupidity.

A repetition that is tiresome in reading or recitation may be acceptable in song; and a good deal of poetry, at least until the eighteenth century, was intended for singing. A group can join in a refrain while the person with leadership, or office, or the best memory, sings the verses. The refrain of a sea shanty often helped the rhythm of the task; repetitive songs helped soldiers to go on marching or enduring wretched conditions.[2] Hymns with refrains such as Alleluyas often contribute to the more emotional forms of religious service.

Benjamin Britten made the *Lyke-Wake Dirge* even more terrifying by a musical setting that brings out the full power of the refrain. Musical settings often *increase*, sometimes greatly, the use of repetition, treating the same words in several ways, as, for instance, in Handel's *Messiah* and other oratorios; we do not normally feel this as tedious reiteration, but as beautiful, and as amplifying the emotional experience.

[1] All statements about folk art need to be taken with a spoonful of salt; there are many different theories.

[2] See, e.g. John Brophy and Eric Partridge, *The Long Trail*, André Deutsch, 1965.

The refrain seems to belong mostly to early poetry or very simple popular poetry; it is rare in more complex, self-conscious, intellectual, poetry that is very far removed from song and ritual. Tennyson's *Mariana* is melodious, delicate, vividly evocative of sight and sound, but its refrain:

> She only said, 'The night is dreary,
> He cometh not,' she said;
> She said, 'I am aweary, aweary,
> I would that I were dead!'

palls somewhat before the end of the poem. To the late-nineteenth-century parodist, Henry Duff Traill, the refrain as used by, for instance William Morris, had become no more than:

> The ballad-burden trick, now known too well,
> . . . turned to scorn, and grown contemptible—
> A too transparent artifice to pass.[1]

Yet, though today a refrain used anything short of brilliantly looks like mere padding, fine poetry that has some incantatory element can use a refrain that is evocative enough; there are the refrains in some of W. B. Yeats's sequence *Words for Music Perhaps*, lines such as:

> A bone wave-whitened and dried in the wind.

or in *The Wild Old Wicked Man* the pictorially and emotionally suggestive:

> Daybreak and a candle-end.

Many poets have kept some of the hypnotic or spell-like

[1] The complete parody may be found in Sir John Squire's anthology of parodies, *Apes and Parrots*, Herbert Jenkins, 1928.

effect of a repeated refrain, yet avoided boredom or the suspicion of meaninglessness by varying the words of the refrain so that they also contribute something to the logical content of the poem. The last line of the first verse of Spenser's elaborate, majestic *Epithalamion* is:

> The woods shall to me answer and my echo ring.

The last line of every subsequent verse includes 'woods', 'answer' and 'echo ring', but with small variations to fit the previous line, in the first sixteen verses; when, after the wedding ceremony, the couple are left alone, there is a shift to:

> Now it is night, ye damsels may be gone,
> And leave my love alone,
> And leave likewise my former lay to sing;
> The woods no more shall answer, nor your echo ring.

and the last lines of the remaining seven verses are variations on this negative command.

Kipling used the varying refrain with skill in such poems as *The Long Trail, The Young British Soldier, Private Ortheris's Song, Back to the Army Again.* G. K. Chesterton often used it in minor comic poems, but with more subtlety and substance (and spell-binding) in *Lepanto* and *The Battle of the Stories.* W. H. Auden has an oddly haunting refrain in the form of a varying dialogue between the two birds in *The Willow-wren and the Stare.*[1] He achieved probably one of the most impressive of all modern manipulations of the varied refrain in his long poem, *The Sea and the Mirror*, based on *The Tempest*, in which various members of the cast speak from their experience, each time followed by a comment from Antonio. First he says:

[1] 'Stare' here means a *starling*.

Your all is partial, Prospero;
My will is all my own:
Your need to love shall never know
Me: I am I, Antonio,
By choice myself alone.

All his subsequent verses keep the same set of rhymes, with sinister effect; in each verse a different item is 'my own'; and a different idea is embedded in a repeated pattern.

This method, used by Auden with great sophistication, is known as *incremental repetition*; this is the repetition of whole stanzas with some of the words changed. In a much simpler fashion this was used in some early ballads, notably *Edward* and *Lord Randal*. The technique is exemplified in the three middle verses of this very early, very simple, religious poem:

I sing of a maiden
That is makeles, (without a mate)
King of all kinges
To her sone sche ches. (chose)
He cam also stille
There his moder was,
As dew in Aprille
That falleth on the grass.
He cam also stille
To his moderes bour, (bower)
As dew in Aprille
That falleth on the flour. (flower)
He cam also stille
There his moder lay,
As dew in Aprille
That falleth on the spray.

Moder and maiden
Was never non but sche;
Well may swich a lady (such)
Godes moder be.

The repetition is incantatory, hypnotic, and emphasizes an exquisite, singular delicacy, quietness, freshness.

A short poem may sometimes have a kind of semi-refrain, in which there is enough repetition to make us expect a complete repetition of the line, and then a modification makes the verse more interesting:

Never weather-beaten sail more willing bent to shore,
Never tired pilgrim's limbs affected slumber more,
Than my weary spright now longs to fly out of my troubled
breast.
O! come quickly, sweetest Lord, and take my soul to rest.

Ever blooming are the joys of Heaven's high Paradise.
Cold age there deafs not our ears, nor vapour dims our eyes.
Glory there the sun outshines, whose beams the blessed
only see.
O! come quickly, glorious Lord, and raise my spright to
thee.

CAMPION

XI INTELLECTUAL FORM

THE MAIN TYPES OF POETRY

> Ay, in the catalogue ye go for men;
> As hounds, and greyhounds, mongrels, spaniels, curs,
> Shoughs, water-rugs, and demi-wolves, are clept
> All by the name of dogs; the valued file
> Distinguishes the swift, the slow, the subtle . . .
>
> SHAKESPEARE: *Macbeth*

Little real sensitivity to poetry is needed to make, for classroom or examination purposes, a passable analysis of the physical form of a poem. Full appreciation requires a grasp of the content of the poem, and an awareness of how rhyme, rhythm, repetition or other formal techniques organize, ornament and reinforce the narrative, argument or emotion.

A detailed classification of poetry in relation to its intellectual or emotional content would require an encyclopaedic volume, and there can be no wholly comprehensive survey, in that the range of possibilities of human expression in poetry, as in all the arts, must approach infinity. The next few chapters can provide only some very elementary notions of some of the most usual poetic methods.

We must bear in mind that, though most poems do have an 'intellectual' content in the everyday sense of the word

—some rational meaning that can be defined and discussed —it is also possible to have poems that we are not meant to understand 'intellectually'. All paraphrase is impertinence and falls short of a total poem, but, while we can fudge up some sort of paraphrase of 'Shall I compare thee to a summer's day?', we can in no sense paraphrase *Jabberwocky*! A poet may intend to subject us to the partly unconscious effect of a group of associations; present us with a curious pattern; tickle us with an interesting noise; play a prank on us; revel in an exuberance; try to share with us some inner experience that cannot be communicated in logical constructions; the possibilities may well be unlimited. We may consider, for instance, some of Edith Sitwell's early poems, Wallace Stevens's *Sea Surface Full of Clouds*, William Empson's *Bacchus* . . . for that matter, *Kubla Khan*.

Poems are often classified in categories which refer partly to the nature of the intellectual content, partly to the techniques used to convey it. A poem may be anything from the brief expression of a single simple mood:

> Lay a garland on my hearse
> Of the dismal yew;
> Maidens, willow branches bear;
> Say, I died true.
>
> My love was false, but I was firm
> From the hour of birth.
> Upon my buried body lie
> Lightly, gentle earth!
>
> JOHN FLETCHER

to something as huge and complex as *Paradise Lost* or Ezra Pound's *The Cantos*. A list of recognized traditional categories of poetry may be useful; but the reader is warned that categories, in art, can seldom be very sharply defined: there will be numerous possibilities of subdivisions, overlaps, exceptions, hybrid and intermediate types—and poems that cannot satisfactorily be assigned to any of the textbook categories.

EPIC

is a narrative poem of great length (a volume in itself); it tells a story of heroic action, in dignified language. The style is usually rather ornate and formal, with elaborate figures of speech, such as long similes; the actual verse form is often relatively simple. Early epics retell national legends; an epic is often thought of as one of a nation's great cultural possessions.
EXAMPLES: Homer's *Iliad* and *Odyssey*; Virgil's *Aeneid*; Milton's *Paradise Lost* and *Paradise Regained*; Spenser's *The Faerie Queene*; Giles Fletcher's *Christ's Victory*; probably Blake's *Milton*, Dante's *Divine Comedy*. There are certain epic conventions, based on Homer, for instance beginning in the middle and telling the earlier part of the story in a flashback; but not all writers of epic observe all the conventions all the time.

MOCK EPIC

is a long narrative poem which treats of un-heroic matter, in comic imitation of some of the practices of serious epic.
EXAMPLES: Pope's *The Rape of the Lock*, Byron's *Don Juan*, Luigi Pulci's *Morgante* (which Byron knew and began to translate), Roy Campbell's *The Georgiad*.

EPIC NARRATIVE

is a poem in the dignified, formal style associated with epic, telling of heroic, important action or suffering, but with one simple action; at what length an epic narrative becomes an epic is uncertain, but it seems reasonable to call a heroic poem an epic narrative if it can be read at one sitting of an hour or two.
EXAMPLES: Chaucer, *The Prioress's Tale, The Clerk's Tale*; Shakespeare, *Venus and Adonis, The Rape of Lucrece*; each narrative in Tennyson's *Idylls of the King*; Matthew Arnold, *Sohrab and Rustum*; John Masefield, *The Everlasting Mercy, Dauber*; C. Day Lewis, *Nabara*.

BALLAD

is a simple, fairly short, narrative poem; its style may not necessarily be naïve or primitive, but it does not have the elaborate figures of speech characteristic of epic and epic narrative.

There are scores of old ballads, anonymous, probably composed long before they were written down, and at their best unforgettably impressive in their very simplicity. There are also numerous more consciously literary ballads by known authors: Wordsworth's *The Last of the Flock, The Thorn, The Idiot Boy*, Coleridge's *The Ancient Mariner*, all found in the volume actually called *Lyrical Ballads*; Oscar Wilde's *Ballad of Reading Gaol*; A. E. Housman's *Hell Gate*, Cowper's comic ballad *John Gilpin*; Auden's *Victor*.

We occasionally find poems exploring further away from the usual ballad tradition that are in some sense ballads, e.g. Dylan Thomas, *Ballad of The Long-legged Bait*, Anne Ridler, *Shooting of his Dear*, Tony Connor, *Mrs Robinson and Mr*

Smith, George Macbeth, *Bedtime Story*, Vernon Scannell, *A Case of Murder*.

A very short poem with narrative content can hardly be called a ballad; we had better call it an anecdote in verse.

FABLE

is one particular kind of narrative, a tale conveying some moral truth or bit of wisdom, in the form of a simple anecdote, usually about animals. It may be in verse or prose. The most famous verse fables are probably the French ones of La Fontaine and the Russian ones of Krylov. Robert Henryson's *Morall Fabillis of Esope the Phrygian* are the most delightful in Britain, if the reader can manage his fifteenth-century Scots. C. Day Lewis's *The Unexploded Bomb* is, though without animals, a kind of modern fable.

The above are all types of narrative. Long non-narrative poems, which may be thought of as *verse essays*, include several recognized types.

DIDACTIC POETRY

'teaching poetry', has the obvious purpose of putting some moral, political, religious or other point of view, or giving some information; it seems reasonable to include also in this category poetry that discusses some problem in a thoughtful way.

EXAMPLES: Sir John Davies: *Nosce Teipsum, Orchestra*; George Herbert, *The Church-Porch*; Alexander Pope, *Essay on Criticism*; Samuel Johnson, *The Vanity of Human Wishes*; Louis MacNeice, *Autumn Journal*. (There is, of course, a didactic *element* in much, perhaps in most, literature; *Paradise Lost* is unmistakably an epic, but its avowed purpose is 'to justify the ways of God to men'; Sir John Betjeman's clever and entertaining *Diary of a Church Mouse*, under cover of elegant fancies, gently rebukes human church members for their want of fervour.)

SATIRE

is always in some sense didactic; it is distinguished by the method of attacking vices, follies or opposing points of view by ridicule and wit.
EXAMPLES: Pope, *The Dunciad*; Byron, *The Age of Bronze*; Dryden, *Absalom and Achitophel*; Auden, *Letter to Lord Byron*; Adrian Mitchell, *Open Day at Porton*; James Fenton, *Open Letter to Richard Crossman*.

The techniques of satire may range from brutally offensive imagery to reticent irony.

EPISTLE

is a letter in verse to some friend or famous person.
EXAMPLES: Pope, *Epistle to Dr Arbuthnot*; Shelley, *Letter to Maria Gisborne*; Auden, *Epistle to a Godson*.

OCCASIONAL VERSE

is any verse written to commemorate a particular event. A poet laureate is expected to produce something for a major State occasion; and many of us try to write verses to greet friends on birthdays or anniversaries. Because real poetic inspiration does not come to order to suit our convenience, much occasional verse is very poor. However, the category includes Andrew Marvell's *Horatian Ode upon Cromwell's Return from Ireland*, Dryden's *Annus Mirabilis*, G. M. Hopkins's *The Wreck of the Deutschland*; Edith Sitwell's *Three Poems of the Atomic Bomb*; T. S. Eliot's *To Walter de la Mare*.

Two special categories of occasional verse are often set apart, and include, probably because they react to two of the most profound human concerns, love and death, much fine poetry: the *epithalamium* and the *elegy*.

The EPITHALAMIUM is a poem commemorating a wedding; Spenser's *Epithalamion* was written to celebrate his own marriage, his *Prothalamion*, in accordance with more usual practice, to celebrate that of two pairs of friends. Among others are Donne's *Epithalamion made at Lincolnes Inne*, Auden's *Epithalamion*, Alex Comfort's *Haste to the Wedding*.

The ELEGY (in modern usage) is a poem mourning the death of an individual, or occasionally a group of people, or all mankind.
EXAMPLES: Gray's *Elegy Written in a Country Churchyard*; Milton's *Lycidas*; Shelley's *Adonais*; Arnold's *Thyrsis*; Auden's *In Memory of Sigmund Freud*; Edwin Muir's *To Ann Scott-Moncrieff*; George Barker's *Letter addressed to the Corpse of Eliot*.

A poem of mourning—usually a fairly short and simple one—may also be called a *dirge* or *lament*.

ODE

is (in modern usage) a fairly long poem, dignified in style, addressed to some person, thing or personified quality, or commemorating some solemn public occasion.

EXAMPLES: Dryden, *Ode for Saint Cecilia's Day*; Keats, *Ode to a Nightingale*; Shelley, *Ode to the West Wind, Hymn to Intellectual Beauty*; Wordsworth, *Ode to Duty*; Tennyson, *Ode on the Death of the Duke of Wellington*; C. Day Lewis, *Ode to Fear.*

LYRIC

This is one of the least sharply defined of all poetic categories. Originally it was a poem to be sung, and today we probably still think of a poem that at least could be set to music as more 'lyrical' than one that could hardly be sung. However, nowadays we may class as a *lyric* almost any short poem expressing the thoughts or feelings of a single speaker. The reader will thus find examples of lyrics in any general anthology of short poems.

EPIGRAM

is a very short, crisp poem, witty and often satirical, usually with a stinging climax.

His whole life is an epigram, smart, smooth, and neatly
    penned,
Plaited quite neat to catch applause, with a hang-noose at the
    end.

BLAKE

Here lies my wife! here let her lie!
Now she's at rest, and so am I.

DRYDEN

Epigrams may also be in prose.

PASTORAL

is a category of verse, prose or even drama; there is a strong pastoral tradition in English poetry. Strictly, pastoral literature presents a setting of (idealized and leisurely) country life, with shepherds and shepherdesses singing, courting or mourning; often real persons and situations were disguised by these rural conventions. Nowadays the term is sometimes applied more generally to literary exploitation of lifestyles that are simpler and so more clearly demonstrate basic realities than our modern, affluent, sophisticated urban life.

EXAMPLES: The *Idylls* of Theocritus and *Eclogues* of Virgil, which gave rise to the European pastoral tradition; both can be read in translation. Spenser, *The Shepheards Calender*; many poems by Sir Philip Sidney; Michael Drayton, *The Shepherd's Garland*; many poems in Herrick's *Hesperides*; William Drummond, *A Pastoral Elegy*. *As You Like It* is to some extent a pastoral poetic drama.

In the broader sense of pastoral we may find very numerous English poems, e.g. Oliver Goldsmith, *The Deserted Village*; Wordsworth, *Michael*; Tennyson, *Enoch Arden*; Edmund Blunden, *Thomasine*.

All the types of poetry mentioned above are what may be called poems of the single voice. An immensely important aspect of English poetry is the verse drama, and there are some minor forms of semi-dramatic poetry.

VERSE DRAMA

may be based on classical models, e.g. Milton, *Samson Agonistes*; Shelley, *Prometheus Unbound*; or have developed

along other lines such as the typical five-act Shakespearian drama with a large cast, complex plot and multiple settings. Blank verse is the most usual verse form, as it is near to the rhythms of common speech; but rhyming couplets and other forms are on occasion used; songs may vary the rhythms; prose may be used for particular purposes.
EXAMPLES: the plays of Shakespeare, Marlowe, Webster, Tourneur, Beaumont and Fletcher, Dryden, Byron, Shelley, Tennyson, Arnold, T. S. Eliot, Louis MacNeice, Christopher Fry, Anne Ridler.

Of relatively recent development is a sub-species of verse drama, the *verse drama for radio*, e.g. Louis MacNeice's *The Dark Tower, Christopher Columbus*.

It is not wise to look at the poetry in a poetic drama simply as poetry with no regard for its dramatic function; the latter may justify some flatness or crudity, far-fetched image or unpleasing sound, as appropriate to a character or situation. It is also a pity if we look at a poetic drama merely as drama without relishing the poetry.

There is also what might be called semi-dramatic poetry.

ECLOGUE

is the traditional form, derived from the classics, of poetic dialogue; originally it was a characteristic form of *pastoral*, e.g. Sidney's dialogue of Strephon and Klaius from his pastoral romance *Arcadia*; Michael Drayton's eclogue 'Late 'twas in June' from *The Shepherd's Garland*; the anonymous *The Nutbrown Maid*; non-pastoral eclogues include Louis MacNeice, *Eclogue from Iceland, Eclogue between the Motherless*.

VERSE DIALOGUE

may be used to cover a rather wider field of miniature drama, e.g. Samuel Daniel, *Ulysses and the Siren*; Browning, *In a Gondola, In a Balcony*; Wordsworth, *The Brothers*; John Press, *A Dialogue*. The purpose of dialogue in verse is usually to clarify some contrast of characters, ideals or ideas.

Finally, there is the

DRAMATIC LYRIC

which is a kind of tiny play using a single voice. Browning has so far been the supreme master of this kind of poem. The poet impersonates someone else and gives an imaginative presentation of the other's point of view.
EXAMPLES: Browning, *My Last Duchess, Caliban upon Setebos, The Bishop Orders his Tomb, Mr Sludge, 'The Medium'*; Tennyson, *St Simeon Stylites, The Spinster's Sweet-Arts*; Yeats, *A Last Confession*; John Heath-Stubbs, *Stone-Age Woman*; Vernon Scannell, *Captain Scuttle Ashore*.

Occasionally poets attempt even more imaginative impersonations, as when in *Eleven from a Bestiary* Robin Skelton speaks with voices devised for lizard, warthog, eagle, slug, spider, goat, bedbug, lobster, spaniel, krait; or George Macbeth in *Scissor-Man* creates a personality for the kitchen scissors!

Though the above critical terms have their usefulness, anyone who reads poetry in any quantity will realize that they by no means cover all existing poems. The student should not over-value critical terms; used without intelligence, or, worse, patronizingly, they can be a substitute for thinking rather than a tool for thinking. The person who uses strings of critical terms pretentiously may well have less real sensitivity to poetry than the person who hears a few splendid lines not heard before, and cannot name the technique, but is haunted all day by the lines themselves.

XII INTELLECTUAL FORM

LOGICAL SEQUENCE

'Is, to dispute well, Logic's chiefest end?'
MARLOWE: *Dr Faustus*

Logic, or the process of correct and disciplined reasoning, is a process entirely of the conscious mind and under our conscious control; it is, if anything, rather opposed to emotion. The greatest poetry may well be that which is highly charged with emotion and at the same time has a firmly organized internal logic; a paraphrase can usually convey only the rational 'meaning' without any of the emotional tension or mysterious effects of imagery. However, the organized structure of a poem is part of its beauty, and a logical sequence, a process of thought, is a large part of the structure.

A narrative poem has as its principal content the story, and a long poem of didactic or satirical intent has a plan that can be worked out much as we may work out a plan before writing an essay. For instance, if we study Pope's *Essay on Criticism* we shall find that the plan is something like this:

1 The importance of sound critical standards:
   (*a*) Good natural taste rare.
   (*b*) But taste can be cultivated.

(*c*) Description of bad and good critics.

2 Follow Nature; the rules are only 'Nature methodiz'd'. Study the classics for examples.

3 Pride is the chief cause of wrong judgments:

(*a*) 'A little learning is a dangerous thing.'

(*b*) We should consider every work of art as a whole.

(*c*) We cannot expect perfection.

(*d*) We should not give all our attention to one aspect of the work of art, as (i) Imagery, (ii) Style, (iii) Rhythm.

(*e*) It is best to avoid extremes.

(*f*) Avoid copying the judgment of others in a servile way.

4 A passage of sympathy for the modern poet and of dispraise for obscenity.

5 A summary of the qualities of a good critic and a bad one.

6 A brief history of Criticism.

The difficulty in grasping the logical sequence is more often felt when dealing with a lyric or other short poem of mood or description. A lyric or other short poem usually has logical structure as one of its components. It need not; this nursery rhyme is hauntingly pretty, but has remarkably little sense:

> I had a little nut-tree, nothing would it bear
> But a silver nutmeg and a golden pear;
> The King of Spain's daughter came to visit me,
> And all was because of my little nut-tree.
> I skipped over water, I danced over sea,
> And all the birds in the air couldn't catch me.

Longer poems may also be difficult of interpretation. For instance, Blake's *Jerusalem*[1] is not a poem whose meaning leaps to the eye at the first reading; here is a brief extract:

Thus sang the Daughters in lamentation, uniting into One.
With Rahab as she turn'd the iron Spindle of destruction.
Terrified at the Sons of Albion they took the Falshood
    which
Gwendolen hid in her left hand; it grew and grew till it
Became a space and an Allegory around the winding Worm.
They named it Canaan and built for it a tender Moon.

The Surrealist artists in both words and pictures depend for their justification on the fact that most of our experiences are not logical and that our thoughts include all kinds of apparently absurd juxtapositions.

If we do not understand the meaning of a poem after several sympathetic readings, we should consider these possibilities in, I think, this order:

1 Should we perhaps be able to understand it if we knew some fact we do not at present know?

For example, some of Chaucer, Shakespeare and Milton is unintelligible without a slight knowledge of medieval astronomy and astrology. Some of Wordsworth is puzzling to one who has no idea of the theories of William Godwin. Classical mythology is essential equipment for any serious student of English literature; many poems require some knowledge of their historical background; twentieth-century poems may assume some knowledge of Freud, Marx, Jung, recent developments in astronomy, medicine, biology, sociology and so on. A poet can hardly expect

[1] The long poem of that title, not the lovely lyric, 'And did those feet in ancient time?' also called 'Blake's Jerusalem'.

everyone to grasp an allusion to, say, rhinolalia aperta or Ganesha, but it is reasonable for the poet to expect readers to be fairly familiar with the more important aspects of contemporary knowledge, or at least to be able to understand a footnote. Ezra Pound and T. S. Eliot sometimes assumed too much; their public will always be somewhat small; but the student should always remember that it is difficult to leave something out of our writing or conversation that is very much a part of our own mental equipment, even when we know that it is by no means common knowledge.

2 Is the poem an allegory or arrangement of symbols that we have missed?

> Having been tenant long to a rich Lord,
> Not thriving, I resolved to be bold,
> And make a suit unto him, to afford
> A new small-rented lease, and cancell th'old.
>
> In heaven at his manour I him sought;
> They told me there, that he was lately gone
> About some land, which he had dearly bought
> Long since on earth, to take possession.
>
> I straight return'd and knowing his great birth,
> Sought him accordingly in great resorts;
> In cities, theatres, gardens, parks and courts:
> At length I heard a ragged noise and mirth
>
> Of theeves and murderers: there I him espied,
> Who straight, *Your suit is granted*, said, and died.
>
> GEORGE HERBERT

This, at first sight, seems a somewhat puzzling poem. The first verse makes perfectly good sense as a statement of someone's business arrangements, but what is 'heaven' doing in the next verse? And why is the rich Lord to be found among thieves and murderers? Has he been murdered? We might suspect a piece of social criticism; all rich lords are thieves and murderers in the sense in which 'property is theft' if they injure their fellow-men; but this lord, so far from being a tyrannical rich man, is kind and grants the tenant's suit even when he is dying and might be pardoned for not thinking about such a matter as someone else's lease. No, this will not do. The reader might be tempted to protest that 'This is not clear; it is not consistent.' I have deliberately cheated the reader by suppressing the title, which is *Redemption*. When we see that the poem is an allegory of the Fall of Man and the death of Christ after His Incarnation, the poem not only makes excellent sense but is very poignant. The intelligent student will be able to work out the details.

We must remember that poetry is often not a matter of literal meaning.

3 Is the poem not intended to be 'understood'? That is, is it intended to have an effect on us entirely through our senses and the use of associations and not by a process of coherent thought? If so, we waste time and spoil the poem by hunting for intellectual meaning.

4 Lastly, and *after every other resort has been tried*, we are entitled to ask: Is this simply a bad poem, a poem that is not to be understood because it is badly written? Such a thing is possible even in the minor works of the great. There are even a few passages of Shakespeare that, as they stand, mean nothing. However, in any work that the ordinary non-specialist student is likely to meet there are far fewer bad or meaningless poems than the hasty or ignorant reader may be tempted to think.

In a short poem that has, as most have, obvious coherent meaning, there are three main kinds of structure, though of course we could go on working out exceptions and subdivisions for another twenty pages. There is the kind in which the poet simply leads up to a climax or summary, the poem in which he turns round on himself with a contradiction and that in which there is what might be called a dialectical development. George Herbert in *Discipline* has such unity in his treatment of the theme of the weakness of Man and the power of God that he nearly repeats the first verse at the end:

Throw away Thy rod,
Throw away Thy wrath.
O my God,
Take the gentle path.

For my heart's desire
Unto Thine is bent.
I aspire
To a full consent.

Not a word or look
I affect to own,
But by book,
And Thy book alone.

Though I fail, I weep.
Though I halt in pace,
Yet I creep
To the throne of grace.

Then let wrath remove.
Love will do the deed:
For with love
Stony hearts will bleed.

Love is swift of foot.
Love's a man of war,
And can shoot,
And can hit from far.

Who can 'scape his bow?
That which wrought on Thee,
Brought Thee low,
Needs must work on me.

Throw away Thy rod,
Though man frailties hath,
Thou art God.
Throw away Thy wrath.

Here there is practically no development of thought; the pathos of the poem is achieved by the very completeness of the mood of trusting humility. Here is a sonnet by Henry Howard, Earl of Surrey, which likewise repeats the idea to strengthen the mood, and works up to an expected climax:

Set me whereas the sun doth parch the green,
Or where his beams do not dissolve the ice;
In temperate heat, where he is felt and seen;
In presence prest of people, mad or wise;
Set me in high, or yet in low degree;
In longest night, or in the shortest day;
In clearest sky, or where clouds thickest be;
In lusty youth, or when my hairs are grey;
Set me in heaven, in earth, or else in hell,
In hill, or dale, or in the foaming flood;
Thrall, or at large, alive whereso I dwell,
Sick, or in health, in evil fame or good,

Hers will I be; and only with this thought
Content myself, although my chance be nought.

On the other hand, a poem may break into two sections with two ideas antithetical to one another. (I do not necessarily mean a direct contradiction, but perhaps a contrast only.)

She is not fair to outward view
As many maidens be,
Her loveliness I never knew
Until she smiled on me;
Oh! then I saw her eye was bright,
A well of love, a spring of light.

But now her looks are coy and cold,
To mine they ne'er reply,
And yet I cease not to behold
The love-light in her eye;
Her very frowns are fairer far
Than smiles of other maidens are.

HARTLEY COLERIDGE

Nay but you, who do not love her,
Is she not pure gold, my mistress?
Holds earth aught—speak truth—above her?
Aught like this tress, see, and this tress,
And this last fairest tress of all,
So fair, see, ere I let it fall?

Because you spend your lives in praising;
To praise, you search the wide world over:
Then why not witness, calmly gazing,
If earth holds aught—speak truth—above her?

Above this tress, and this, I touch
But cannot praise, I love so much!

ROBERT BROWNING

Or here is a more direct contradiction from Sir Philip Sidney; I quote the first and last verses only, as the second and third verses are allegorical enlargements upon the first:

Ring out you bells, let mourning shows be spread;
For Love is dead:
All Love is dead, infected
With plague of deep disdain:
Worth, as naught worth, rejected,
And Faith fair scorn doth gain.
From so ungrateful fancy,
From such a female frenzy,
From them that use me thus,
Good Lord, deliver us!

Alas, I lie: rage hath this error bred;
Love is not dead;
Love is not dead, but sleepeth
In her unmatched mind,
Where she his counsel keepeth,
Till due deserts she find.
Therefore, from so vile fancy,
To call such wit a frenzy,
Who Love can temper thus,
Good Lord, deliver us!

These poems may or may not be more beautiful, but for intellectual experience they are much fuller than the previous pair. Sonnets very often have this kind of contrast in them; the student should examine some of Shakespeare's sonnets; I do not quote any of these, as they ought to be available on everyone's bookshelf. In general, the poem of a single main idea tends rather to make us share the emotion with the writer, the poem of contrast rather to make us join the writer in thinking about the subject; but, like all generalizations, this can be misleading.

The third and most complicated kind of intellectual structure is what might be called dialectical, or a contradiction resolved. Let me illustrate this idea frivolously and crudely, so that I need not pull a beautiful example to pieces:

I am very fond of good food, and am, as might be expected, somewhat fatter than I would wish to be. I sometimes cut down my food in order to lose some of my excess fat. It will be imagined that this sometimes gives rise to mental conflict, and, though the theme is not important enough to give rise to great creative stresses and strains, I can write about it. If I think, now, of food, my first reaction is to contemplate the prospect with delight:

> O how I love to sit and eat
> Hors-d'oeuvres and soup and fish and meat
> With vegetables, then a sweet!
> O what a treat!

Here is a *Rhapsody before Lunch.*[1] I will now add another verse, thus making the poem into the second type, the poem of contrast or contradiction:

> But as I gaze upon my plate
> I know it is my hapless fate,
> Eating, to do the thing I hate,
> To put on weight!

[1] Not, I had better add, my usual lunch!

Instead of calling it *Rhapsody before Lunch*, I shall now call it *The Glutton's Dilemma*. The poem still has unity in the contrast, but unity of quite a different kind. Now, if I think the paltry subject of my shape is worth so much attention, I may choose to add a third verse suggesting one of the three possible solutions to the dilemma—to choose grace, to choose grub, or to decide that current ideas of beauty are wrong and to resign myself to my size. Whatever solution I choose, the poem will then be an arrangement of ideas that could be symbolized by the equation $a + b = c$.

Pass me a second butter-pat!
I know I never shall be flat!
I choose to eat although I'm fat,
And that is that!

This is not a real poem on any usual definition, but I hope it makes clear what I mean by a dialectical arrangement. Such a poem will not, of course, necessarily, be a poem of three verses or even lines in some multiple of three; the same space is not always given to each idea. For further examples the student may like to look at Shakespeare's Sonnets numbers VII, XIX, XXXIII, XLVIII, XCI and CX. Here is a beautiful example from Henry Vaughan:

The Shower

'Twas so; I saw thy birth. That drowsy lake
From her faint bosom breathed thee, the disease
Of her sick waters and infectious ease.
But now at even,
Too gross for Heaven,
Thou fall'st in tears, and weep'st for thy mistake.

Ah! it is so with me. Oft have I pressed
Heaven with a lazy breath, but fruitless this
Pierced not; love only can with quick access
Unlock the way,
When all else stray,
The smoke and exhalations of the breast.

Yet, if as thou dost melt, and with thy train
Of drops make soft the Earth, my eyes could weep
O'er my hard heart, that's bound up and asleep;
Perhaps at last,
Some such showers past,
My God would give a sunshine after rain.

This kind of highly logical structure is most likely to be found in the 'metaphysical' poets of the seventeenth century, of whom Henry Vaughan and John Donne are two, and in some of the best contemporary poets, who have a good deal in common with the 'metaphysicals', having some of the same intellectual toughness. Edwin Muir uses antithetical structure in many of his poems, e.g. *The Recurrence, The Good Man in Hell, The Castle.* The reader may also study Muir's three-stage structure in *The Three Mirrors* or *The Myth.*

XIII INTELLECTUAL FORM

THE USE OF ASSOCIATIONS

> I never see thy face but I think upon hell-fire and Dives that lived in purple; for there he is in his robes, burning, burning.
>
> SHAKESPEARE: *Henry IV*, Pt. 1

Early discussion of poetry almost entirely omitted the study of the effect of associations, and it is only in comparatively recent years that any attempt has been made to study them as systematically as, say, prosody has been studied. Yet these are very important features of poetry.

Much of our learning is done by association of one object or idea with another; all students find that lists of unrelated facts are far harder to learn than groups of related facts. If you wish to remember something, you may tie a knot in your handkerchief, in the hope that every time you take out your handkerchief to blow your nose you will be reminded of your unaccomplished task. If you have to remember some fact such as a date, you will remember it far more easily by making up a jingle about it; and if you cannot think where you put your pen, your best way to find it is probably to think quietly about the events of the day until some train of thought leads you to where you last had the pen.

Associations also have great power to arouse emotions, a fact which makes them, at times, highly dangerous; the cunning use of associations is behind most advertising, much electioneering and a great deal of successful emotional tyranny at home and further afield. Certain words, such as *England, family, love, peace, God, freedom, moral*, may be so heavily loaded with emotion for us that we are unable to consider problems in whose context these words are mentioned without becoming highly unreasonable and intolerant. On the other hand, some words are not easy to pronounce in public because the associations are painful, sordid or embarrassing. If you mention fly-paper to someone whose sole experience of fly-paper is for catching flies, there will be no emotional reaction; but if you mention it to someone who a few hours before had publicly been caught by the hair in a fly-paper and made to look foolish, they are likely to blush; if you mention it solemnly enough before someone who has so far successfully concealed a murder committed with arsenic soaked off fly-papers, they may well turn pale or faint. The three patterns of association in the individual mind are quite different.

Association in poetry must obviously depend for its effect on things that are common to many people, not things that are suggested to a very few individuals only. Indeed, a poem is sometimes spoilt by a wrong association due to some change in the meaning of a word. I hope I may be forgiven for admitting that the line:

> As if the earth in fast thick pants were breathing

from *Kubla Khan*, used to give me, not the intended picture of a great heaving globe, but a picture of an earth something like the world-on-little-legs of the cartoonists, looking hot and uncomfortable in over-substantial underclothes![1] Fortunately, a great many associations are to be found in most minds that are sufficiently intelligent and well-furnished to have any associations at all. People of very low intelligence do not enjoy poetry anyway.

A great deal of the effect of poetry depends on these mental connections. If I speak of a *lily*, it suggests purity, but nowadays, thanks to the pictures of the pre-Raphaelites and to Gilbert and Sullivan's *Patience*, it may also suggest a rather sickly, over-refined kind of purity that is more decadent than honest earthiness. 'Cold lilies' would be a safer phrase than 'sweet lilies'. If I speak of a mouse, the atmosphere is one of smallness, friendliness and probably triviality. That is why Falstaff talking to his recruits is so comical when he addresses Feeble, who has said bravely: 'I will do my good will, sir; you can have no more.' 'Well said, good woman's tailor! Well said, courageous Feeble! thou wilt be as valiant as the wrathful dove or the most magnanimous mouse.'—*Henry IV*, part II.

On the other hand, if I mention slimy slugs and writhing worms, the reader is prepared for something revolting.

A woman's hair, if long and healthy, is beautiful, and is fascinating to most men, yet it is not luminous, nor even very bright by reflection; but when Lovelace says:

> Do not then wind up that light
> In ribbands, and o'ercloud in night
> Like the sun in's early ray;
> But shake your head, and scatter day!

[1] The reader of poetry should dismiss all such inappropriate associations. The teacher, however, has to watch for them!

we are given, by the associations of brilliant daybreak, a mental picture of a beautiful woman shaking out a mass of golden locks so radiantly bright that they seem to be dripping with golden light. It is a lovely image, though true only for a lover.

The same word does not always carry the same associations, and may carry two or more associations at once; ambiguous associations are often important in some of the most exciting poetry. *Blood* can mean 'rank', 'aristocracy':

> The glories of our blood and state
> Are shadows, not substantial things. . . .
>
> SHIRLEY

> A shielded scutcheon blush'd with blood of queens and
> kings.
>
> KEATS

It can instead mean 'murder', 'war', 'atrocity':

> It will have blood, they say; blood will have blood;
> Stones have been known to move and trees to speak;
> Augurs and understood relations have
> By maggot-pies and choughs and rooks brought forth
> The secret'st man of blood.
>
> SHAKESPEARE: *Macbeth*

It can suggest human lust and the instinctive life—we know the phrase 'hot blood' for the part of our lives during which, we most readily fall in love:

> I do know
> When the blood burns, how prodigal the soul
> Lends the tongue vows. . . .
>
> SHAKESPEARE: *Hamlet*

and it can, in two lines only, horribly suggest both at once:

> Oh, my greatest sin lay in my blood!
> Now my blood pays for't.
>
> WEBSTER: *The White Devil*

The word can also be divorced from its associations of death and evil to suggest the flush on the face of a young girl:

> Hood my unmanned blood, bating in my cheeks. . . .
>
> SHAKESPEARE: *Romeo and Juliet*

Roses suggest love and a certain softness or luxuriance; gold suggests riches, hardness or prestige; purple may suggest rank, or sacrifice, authority or blood or mourning; green is the colour of spring and hope or in some contexts may remind us instead of the ugly colours of putrefaction; the sun is generally beneficent:

> The sun, whose beams most glorious are
> Rejecteth no beholder. . . .
>
> Sun of my soul, thou Saviour dear. . . .

but can also be sinister when associated with the deadly sun of the desert:

> The sun says, 'I will suck your bones
> And afterwards bury you.'
>
> SIDNEY KEYES: *The Wilderness*

The associations of a word thus depend very largely on the context. Words like *roses, blood, wine, bread, hair, hands, stars, bells, worms, home, mother*, that are in everyday use and heavily charged with associations are more likely to be effective in poetry than such words as *iambic, pethidine, mollusc, rotation, detergent, hydrogen, matriculation,* whose meaning is so sharply defined that there is little room for a haze of associations around them. On the other hand, the evocative power even of *rose* or *cross* may fade from over-use; the poetic vocabulary has to be extended. In our own time, perhaps Auden above all, but also Pound, Eliot, Graves, Empson, Amis, Larkin and many others have brought fresh words and idioms into poetic use.

French, and to a lesser extent English, classicist critics such as Samuel Johnson tried to teach writers that there were limitations on the vocabulary proper to poetry, imposed by considerations of dignity. When a translation of *Othello* was first performed in France, the word *mouchoir* (handkerchief) nearly provoked a riot; so common an object was quite beneath the dignity of poetry and should have been mentioned in a long-winded circumlocution. Shakespeare has been blamed for making Heaven, in *Macbeth, peep* through the *blanket* of the dark, on the grounds that this was undignified. The idea that some words were more suited to poetry than others was probably an early consciousness of the power of a word's associations, and there is enough truth in it to make its acceptance understandable. The handkerchief of Desdemona and the 'blanket of the dark' are acceptable enough to us, but the best of poets might still have some difficulty in introducing such a word as *kippers* or *peanuts* into a poem that was lyrical without humour or irony.[1] Nowadays it is safer to say that all words are suitable for use in poetry, however crude and common, rare, or technical, provided that their associations are appropriate to the con-

[1] Louis MacNeice successfully used many words such as *peanuts, pretzels, beer, clams, queues,* in his fine ironical poem *Bar-Room Matins.*

text or, if they have a number of different associations, that the force of the context is sufficient to keep the unwanted ones out of our minds. On the whole—if we are to judge from literary history—anything that narrows the scope of poetry is likely to be a mistake.

This importance of associations is one of the principal differences between prose and poetry; I am not sure that it is not more important even than the use of metrical pattern. All metaphor depends on associations, and metaphor is the very life of poetry; metaphor (and kindred modes of speech such as simile and personification) is imagery. We reason in prose by analogy, which is a kind of simile:

'If you exercise your mind with literature, philosophy and science, it will grow broader and more able, just as if you exercise your body muscles will develop and you will be stronger.'

'A spiral staircase is one that goes round and round like a corkscrew, instead of up at an angle.'

But such explanations are useful only to help us to understand the fact; they are not emotionally exciting. Analogy in reasoning elucidates; metaphor in poetry enriches. We may already know the fact; indeed, if we do not we shall probably not gain the maximum excitement from the poem; but something is added to our experience by seeing it expressed in an image. No one needs to be told that time flies fast and that we never have time enough to do all we wish; but when we read Marvell's great lines:

> But at my back I always hear
> Time's winged chariot hurrying near;
> And yonder all before us lie
> Desarts of vast eternity.

it does add something to our sense of urgency. Here is a simile—the simplest form of image—used by Landor to elucidate, actually to make us see something in a new light.

On Catullus

Tell me not what too well I know
About the bard of Sirmio. . . .
Yes, in Thalia's son
Such stains there are . . . as when a Grace
Sprinkles another's laughing face
With nectar, and runs on.

This is very like the use of analogy in prose; yet the choice of words, making a picture, enriches the idea. The vices of Catullus, which were sensual, are attributed by association to pagan vitality and placed in a setting of fresh youth and beauty. The sensual vices (so-called) are not repulsive in the young and beautiful, so we feel we can accept this explanation, though in cold fact it is no explanation at all.

Let us take a short and fairly simple lyric and study the use of associations in it:

Music, when soft voices die,
Vibrates in the memory—
Odours, when sweet violets sicken,
Live within the sense they quicken.

Rose leaves, when the rose is dead,
Are heaped for the beloved's bed;
And so thy thoughts when thou art gone,
Love itself shall slumber on.

SHELLEY

Now, if we are to consider merely the rational meaning of this, it is platitudinous: 'We are able to recollect the experiences of listening to music and smelling violets; dead roses can be used in the house; in some such way, when you are gone, your thoughts will be something on which Love can rest.' This is sorry stuff and has lost all the wistfulness and grace of the poem.

The poem suggests far more than it says; its title is *To* ——, evidently one of the women idealistically loved by Shelley. The music is vocal music, which is more intimately personal than instrumental music; the 'soft voice' is part of a woman's physical attraction, especially for a refined and spiritual man such as Shelley; indeed, the use of the word 'soft' suggests that the poet is thinking of speech as much as music, for too soft a voice is useless for singing. Violets are associated with modesty and fragrance and are a flower made more precious by needing to be sought. (We can also think of the violets in Donne's *The Extasie* and the 'beds of violets blue and fresh-blown roses washed in dew' of Milton; the violet had earlier literary associations of love and happiness.) 'Sicken' is a more human word than 'wither'; it suggests almost that the withering of violets is not necessary, that it is an illness rather than the normal state of things, or else, conversely, we may take it to mean that our illnesses and death and the disillusionments of love are like the fading of flowers, natural and easy. The rose is very rich with associations of love, happiness and festivity:

> For nothing this wide universe I call
> Save thee, my rose; in it thou art my all.
>
> SHAKESPEARE

> It was roses, roses, all the way.
>
> BROWNING

The rose leaves could just as well, factually, have gone into a jar to make fragrant pot-pourri, and indeed the cynic might argue that rose leaves would not be comfortable in bed; but the 'bed' is used to suggest some kind of loving ritual (as with altar flowers, perhaps?) and to take up the picture of Love slumbering. The suggestion of Love slumbering is also that Love may again be awakened. If we take into account all these associations and implications the poem becomes much more subtle and beautiful.

In order to be effective, associations must be generally comprehensible. Everyone agrees that roses, violets and music are agreeable things. Sometimes when a reader does not appreciate a poem fully it is because some of the associations are not affecting him. This may be the poet's fault for using associations that even an educated and sensitive person cannot be expected to grasp. More often it is the fault of circumstance because the association has become unfamiliar with the passage of time, or is not now emotionally charged. More often still it is the reader's fault for having inadequate general knowledge, experience, or imagination. It is, I think, the business of a poet to choose images that are comprehensible to his audience[1] if he wants an audience. But it should be added that the poet has a perfect right to choose his audience. T. S. Eliot and Robert Burns are both very fine poets; Eliot demands a much higher standard of culture from his readers; but he is entirely justified in writing for a smaller audience. There will always be some people too stupid, lazy or ignorant to enjoy any poem, even a simple one; the poet is expected merely to

[1] Not always intellectually, in the sense that the poem can be paraphrased word-for-word; the morning-bright Apollo forbid so narrow an idea of 'understanding'!

avoid making impossible demands on the kind of audience for which he is writing. (In a sense the poet is always writing mostly to himself; but if we are studying his work it must have been published, which implies that he wishes for some audience.)

Let me again take a flippant example. I am very short-sighted, and am helpless without the glasses I wear all day. Suppose I wished to write a poem of dignity and pathos about some terrible political problem with which my country was faced, and how difficult it was to see what to do; I might, drawing a vital image from my own daily experience, say something like this:

> Confused as is the room to waking eyes,
> Early, before the spectacles are on,
> The borders blurred, the detail indistinct,
> All dangers seeming larger than they are. . . .

This is an excellent image for *me*; but for someone who has faultless eyesight and has never experienced a blurring of vision it is nearly meaningless. Actually ordinary human sympathy probably extends so far; most people are aware of the predicaments of spectacle-wearers; but the image would lack all the vividness and realism it has for me. Everybody has at some time looked out through a rain-smeared window on to a dark night, and it would be much better to say, using an image that is intelligible both to the normally sighted and to me, that is therefore successful as *communication*:

> Confused as darkening gardens are outside,
> When heavy rain channels the window pane,
> And all the trees take on a sinister size
> In blurs and gathering opacity.

I have said that we must be careful not to put a word in a context where it carries the inappropriate associations, but some of the most exciting associations may very well be ambiguous. One of the continually exciting things about life is that everything is a part of everything else, and associations in poetry often heighten this awareness. For example, in Andrew Marvell's *The Garden* we find these two lines:

> When we have run our passion's heat,
> Love hither makes his best retreat.

There is a surprising amount of implication packed into these two lines. 'Heat' is here obviously a heat in a race, since we 'run' it; we have finished that part of our life in which passion is important. But passion is itself, in literary parlance, 'heat', both in a refined metaphorical sense and as when we speak of an animal being 'in heat'. 'Retreat' suggests defeat in battle—Love surrenders, gives in, to the inevitable; but it also suggests, and would probably do so much more strongly to the very religion-conscious seventeenth century, a religious 'retreat'—a retirement from the world to monastery or convent in order to contemplate. Thus the couplet has four possible meanings and all of them are really to be felt together. To pursue such ambiguous associations is a very exciting part of criticism.

Association can also be used ironically. Wilfred Owen, in his poems of protest at the horror and cruelty of war, frequently does this, as here, describing a young boy with a gun:

> Lend him to stroke those blind, blunt bullet-heads
> Which long to nuzzle in the hearts of lads.

'Stroke' and 'nuzzle' suggests an affectionate relationship with a pet, and the implications are that the boy ought to be playing with harmless pets rather than familiarizing himself with lethal weapons, also that he is making a pet of his gun, treating it as a toy because he is too young to understand his situation.

The sting of satire is often sharpened by the use of association, even though completely unfair. Byron in *English Bards and Scotch Reviewers* writes of Wordsworth:

> Thus, when he tells the tale of Betty Foy,
> The idiot mother of 'an idiot boy';
> A moon-struck, silly lad, who lost his way,
> And like his bard confounded night with day;
> So close on each pathetic part he dwells,
> And each adventure so sublimely tells,
> That all who view 'the idiot in his glory'
> Conceive the bard the hero of the story.

Now, this is undoubtedly funny and clever, but it is most unfair, for it manages to imply that Wordsworth is himself an idiot, with no more evidence given than that the poet once wrote a poem about an idiot boy. (It is not even accurate, for the boy's mother was not an idiot.) All the epithets applied to the idiot and his mother are obliquely being flung at Wordsworth himself. Satire is meant to be aggressive and must be allowed to make some rash assumptions and exaggerations; often the less fair satire is the funnier it is; but we must distinguish the real criticism in satire from the clever use of associations and implications.

XIV INTELLECTUAL FORM

THE TWO MAIN PATTERNS OF IMAGERY

All garlanded with carven imag'ries
KEATS: *Eve of St Agnes*

In general a poem may have a series of images that support or contradict one another, or a single dominant image on which the sequence and structure of the poem depend. Burns's *A Red, Red Rose* expresses passionate love by a series of simple and beautiful hyperboles; his effect is achieved by an accumulation of images that are not closely related to one another.[1]

O my luve is like a red, red rose,
That's newly sprung in June;
O my luve is like the melodie,
That's sweetly play'd in tune.

As fair art thou, my bonnie lass,
So deep in luve am I;
And I will luve thee still, my dear,
Till a' the seas gang dry.

[1] The student who has read the previous chapter attentively will find much food for thought in the associations.

Till a' the seas gang dry, my dear,
And the rocks melt wi' the sun;
And I will love thee still, my dear,
While the sand o' life shall run.

And fare-thee-weel, my only luve!
And fare-thee-weel awhile!
And I will come again, my luve,
Though it were ten thousand mile.

Collections of unrelated images may also be found in Nashe's *Adieu; farewell Earth's bliss*, Crashaw's *Wishes for the Supposed Mistress*, and Shelley's *When the Lamp is Shattered.*

Another type of poem, which makes a very different impression on the mind, uses a single central, dominant image and builds the whole structure of the poem around it. In George Herbert's *Love* the experience of divine love is shown as the shy attendance of a consciously unworthy guest at a feast:

Love bade me welcome; yet my soul drew back,
Guilty of dust and sin.
But quick-eyed Love, observing me grow slack
From my first entrance in,
Drew nearer to me, sweetly questioning
If I lacked anything.

A guest, I answered, worthy to be here.
Love said, You shall be he.
I, the unkind, ungrateful? Ah, my dear,
I cannot look on thee.
Love took my hand and smiling made reply,
Who made the eyes but I?

> Truth, Lord, but I have marred them; let my shame
> Go where it doth deserve.
> And know you not, says Love, who bore the blame?
> My dear, then I will serve.
> You must sit down, said Love, and taste my meat.
> So I did sit and eat.

This is, in a sense, a small allegory, though the term is more often given to a larger piece of work. Clearly, here, Love is Divine Love, probably Christ as Redeemer, and the unworthy guest is George Herbert, aware of his sins; but we need not try to find allegorical meanings for the taking of the hand or the making of the eyes; ''twere to consider too curiously, to consider so.' It is possible that the poem refers to the actual partaking of the Holy Communion, but it might equally well be a poem about some other mystical experience of God outside orthodox ritual. I, who am not a Christian, can still be moved by its beauty, because I know that even human love, at its best, is like this, this unconditional generosity of spirit that takes no notice of our deserving. The refusal to produce images which are very limited in their application has probably widened the audience that can appreciate the poem.

An image may also recur in a long poem or a dramatic poem so often as to be its dominant image; its choice is very significant. It has been pointed out that this is often true of the plays of Shakespeare: the image of torture and physical cruelty recurs in *King Lear*; darkness and blood in *Macbeth*; disease in *Hamlet*; animals and the sea in *Othello*. The relationship of these dominant images to the plot is obvious.

Many poets have favourite images that recur in their poems. Shelley's works are full of friendly snakes, the sea and the sky; the poems of Donne, more earthy and more rational, are full of images drawn from science and theology. Wordsworth has a powerful favourite symbol of some solitary figure in impressive natural surroundings —the Leech Gatherer, Lucy Gray, the soldier in *The Prelude*; Keats is full of images of texture, colour and sensation. In the poems of A. E. Housman a hanging frequently plays a part, though we know of no biographical reason. W. H. Auden has images of children, Roy Campbell of red, violence, and the beasts and birds of South Africa; James Kirkup favours the sea and mirrors; spindles and gyres turn among the gold and blood of W. B. Yeats and at one time C. Day Lewis was using much imagery drawn from railways. The student should look out for other examples. This is usually because poets create their own personal mythology. Similarly many poets have favourite words that recur with sometimes embarrassing frequency: Shelley's *skiey* and *crystal*, Swinburne's *roses* and *tears* and *sin*, Pope's *wit*, Blake's *howling*, Wordsworth's *solitary*, give a clue to their interests.

This is not merely, however, evidence of the general capacity of human beings for repeating themselves. The poet chooses an image to illustrate his own experience for himself, as well as to pass it on to others. The imagery of a poem is often not so much like a pattern chosen for embroidery or the few well-chosen words arranged for a public speech, as like a myth or the illogical but curiously exciting pictures seen in dreams. I once heard a distinguished young woman biologist read some poetry that she had written; it was quite good poetry, though she refused to publish it; she read it with sincerity and then rejected it with scorn, saying that the images were all the usual dream-symbols mentioned by Freud. This was true, but did not seem to me to spoil her poems. Various students of literature who are also psychologists have pointed out the resemblance of much poetic language to dreams, myths and the visionary experiences of primitive men.[1] The poet does not always consciously choose his image; the image may choose him. The psychologist will say that an image that insists on being used has sprung from the unconscious mind; the romantic idealist will say that the poet is divinely inspired. On this difference of opinion I can do no better than quote the great wisdom of George Bernard Shaw, who, when the Inquisitors tell Saint Joan that the 'voices' she hears come from her imagination, makes her say: 'Of course; that is how the messages of God come to us.' When a poet has an obvious dominant personal image, the psychologist can usually suggest a reason, but this does not make the poem any less good. In general, it seems that the poems that are most widely appreciated are those whose images are present in the minds of most people. A poem depicting the forces of evil as a great snake would be accepted by most Westerners; a poem of equal merit depicting them as an enormous frog might not be accepted so readily; a lamb would be impossible.

Sometimes we feel the effect of a poem more by relaxing and letting it sink in than by studying it intellectually. This is true of much of Swinburne, Shelley, Blake, Poe, Whitman and Spenser. The images affect us long before we have grasped the intellectual meaning. I have a curious little memory of this. As a quite small child, I think of about eight, I read *A Midsummer Night's Dream* and was so terrified by the lines:

[1] See Herbert Read: 'Myth, Dream and Poem' in his *Collected Literary Criticism*, Faber & Faber, 1938.

> I'll believe as soon
> The whole earth may be bor'd, and that the moon
> May through the centre creep, and so displease
> Her brother's noontide with the Antipodes.

that I lay awake at night with obscure pictures of darkness and horror multiplying in my head. *A Midsummer Night's Dream* is not the play one would hesitate to give to little girls! But, with no understanding of 'antipodes' and not much understanding of the words at all, I did receive some disturbingly strong impression of the whole order of Nature being upset. I still find the idea terrifying now that I know what it means, and occasionally have dreams of double suns, distorted moons and strange new features in the sky. However, probably a really great poem is one in which the image, while it has an immediate and powerful emotional effect, will also bear intellectual analysis. In Otway's *Venice Preserved* the heroine goes mad and makes an exit speaking incoherently of

> Lutes, laurels, seas of milk and ships of amber.

This is reasonable enough to suggest the ravings of a stage madwoman; it makes no sense, it sounds pleasant and the vague suggestion of glory, music and plenty is suitable to the high rank of the personages. Yet, compared with the ravings of Lear, this seems poor, synthetic stuff. The student should turn to *King Lear*, Act iv, scene vi, and examine Lear's mad speeches in detail. Every image, pretty, grandiose or repulsive, has significance; minute intellectual analysis of its implications (including the stage business implied) is possible. For the greatest poetic excitement, we need imagery that strikes directly at the unconscious mind and is also worth analysis by the conscious reasoning mind.

It seems likely that poets writing before the development of depth psychology and related methods of literary criticism were less self-conscious about their imagery than most, probably, are today. Allegory was worked out in minute detail and with great care; massive epic similes provided 'purple patches'; but some impressive images of early poetry give the impression of having been discovered almost by accident; they have the dew upon them:

When the nightegale singes, the wodes waxen grene;
Lef and gras and blosme springes in Averil, I wene,
And love is to myn herte gon with one spere so kene:
Night and day my blood it drinkes, myn herte deth me
tene.[1]

Anonymous Mediaeval Love-Poem

Brightness falls from the air.

NASHE

The maid she went to the well to washe,
Dew fell off her lily-white flesh.

Ballad

Then Mary plucked a cherry
As red as the blood;
Then Mary went home
With her heavy load.

Old Carol

More pale she was, when she sought my grace,
Than primrose pale and wan;

[1] *waxen*, become; *blosme*, blossom; *Averil*, April; *deth me tene*, causes me pain.

And redder than rose her ruddy heart's blood
That down my broadsword ran.

Jellon Graeme

O the wind is longer nor the way
And love is deeper nor the sea.

The Riddling Knight

Sing levy dew, sing levy dew,
The water and the wine;
The seven bright gold wires
And the bugles they do shine.

A New Year Carol

The student might also think of the queer excitement of the full version of *Green Grow the Rushes-O* with its half-understood primitive symbols, *Maiden in the Moor Lay*, and this nursery rhyme, not now much used among children:

This is the Key of the Kingdom:
In that Kingdom is a city;
In that city is a town;
In that town there is a street;
In that street there winds a lane;
In that lane there is a yard;
In that yard there is a house;
In that house there waits a room;
In that room an empty bed;
And on that Bed a basket—
A Basket of Sweet Flowers,
Of Flowers, of Flowers,
A Basket of Sweet Flowers.

Flowers in a Basket;
Basket on the bed;
Bed in the chamber;
Chamber in the house;
House in the weedy yard;
Yard in the winding lane;
Lane in the broad street;
Street in the high town;
Town in the city;
City in the Kingdom;
This is the Key of the Kingdom,
Of the Kingdom this is the Key.

A whole chapter could be given to commenting upon this amazing poem; completely unsophisticated and having very possibly happened by 'accident', it has some symbols of great richness.

One might argue that one aspect of the Romantic Revival was an attempt to return to spontaneity in image-finding, after the evocative scholarship of Milton, the intellectuality of Dryden, the studied complexities of Donne and other metaphysical poets, the balanced elegance of Pope; the idea of 'back to nature' tends to recur in cultural history.

Modern urban people, in the richest countries with the least oppressive governments, can now enjoy comforts, leisure, choices, entertainment, access to knowledge, variety in personal relationships, liberty in spiritual quests, general freedom in individuality, undreamed of in any previous century; and yet we tend to feel we have lost something. If pushed to explain our apparent freakish thanklessness, and articulate, we might perhaps say something about simplicity and spontaneity.

In fact most of us are probably allowed more scope for spontaneity than most people had in any previous epoch; but modern life and thought are certainly far from simple. There are kinds of poetry that can no longer be written, or, at least, taken seriously. Those who dislike twentieth-century poetry for being over-intellectual, too complex, too self-conscious, may be explaining correctly why this poetry does not appeal to them. They cannot, however, tell poets how to write like mediaeval songsters or Elizabethan lyricists, when their much greater general knowledge is also essentially a knowledge of the vast complexity of the cosmos, nature, human society and the human personality. It also includes new and disturbingly complicated awarenesses about the nature and functioning of language, and a vast inheritance of previous poetry and analysis of poetry. The modern poet is heavily burdened by the complexity and ambiguity of life today; but he or she is also immeasurably enriched. However much refreshment we may find in an older poetry, we shall find little nourishment for modern man in a contemporary poetry that evades contemporary consciousness.

All poets have to try to come to terms with the experience of their own epoch, even if their main reaction is to protest about it. This is nothing new. To give one example only, Tennyson in *In Memoriam* was trying to sort out some of his thoughts and feelings, not only in the universal experience of bereavement, but also on some of the developments in knowledge and speculation that had disturbed thinking people only in his lifetime.

The sentimentality that laments that awe and wonder and mystery have been taken from life by modern knowledge is rather like a childish dismay on finding that Santa Claus is only Daddy, when the real mystery of parental love is far more interesting, wonderful and inexhaustible than a minor traditional rite. Poets writing today have to find new methods, offer new experiences to readers, just as poets have had to do through all the centuries; but our own epoch offers enormous storehouses full of new material from which poets can create new imagery.

XV SOME TRADITIONAL VERSE FORMS

Blessed be all metrical rules that forbid automatic responses,
force us to have second thoughts, free from the fetters of Self.

W. H. AUDEN, *Shorts II*

A list of traditional verse forms with recognized names may be useful, though the reader should remember that the definitions refer to the basic metre only, and diverse adjustments of the variations may produce appreciably different effects; and that a great many more verse forms have been used, but have not been named.

BLANK VERSE

Definition: A sequence of unrhymed iambic pentameters.
EXAMPLES: Most of Shakespeare's dramatic verse; Milton, *Paradise Lost*; Cowper, *The Task*; Wordsworth, *The Prelude*; Sir John Betjeman, *Beside the Seaside*.

Blank verse is the principal form for English dramatic poetry. A rhythm common in everyday speech, it allows variations that can give it many different tones.

COUPLET

Definition: a pair of lines, in any metre, rhyming. Couplets may be long or short, solemn or skipping. An important distinct variety is the

HEROIC COUPLET

Definition: Iambic pentameter lines rhyming in pairs. Although termed 'heroic' the form is most commonly used in English for satirical or didactic poetry. It was a favoured form in the eighteenth century, but has never gone entirely out of fashion. The heroic couplet is often 'closed', i.e. avoids enjambement.
EXAMPLES: Chaucer, *Prologue*; Pope, *Essay on Criticism*; Johnson, *The Vanity of Human Wishes*; George Crabbe, *The Village*; Roy Campbell, *Veld Eclogue—The Pioneers*.
Another widely used couplet form is

OCTOSYLLABICS

Definition: Though 'octosyllabics' could mean any form of eight-syllable line, conventionally the term applies to iambic tetrameters rhyming in couplets.
EXAMPLES: Butler, *Hudibras*; Scott, *Marmion*; Andrew Marvell, *The Garden*; Byron, *The Prisoner of Chillon*; Keats, *The Eve of St Mark*; John Masefield, *The Everlasting Mercy*; Auden, *New Year Letter*.

TRIPLET

Definition: A group of three lines, in any metre, rhyming.
EXAMPLES: Tennyson, *The Two Voices*; Kathleen Raine,

Passion; Kipling, *Dedication* from *Barrack-room Ballads*.

Sets of three are not common in English poetry, but an important three-line form is

TERZA RIMA

Definition: Iambic pentameters rhyming aba bcb cdc ded efe and so on, ending with a quatrain or couplet to avoid leaving one word unrhymed. The form is taken from Dante's *Divine Comedy*. It is not very common in English poetry. EXAMPLES: Byron, *The Prophecy of Dante* (appropriately!); Shelley, *The Triumph of Life, Ode to the West Wind, Prince Athanase*; Thomas Hardy, *The Burghers*; Edwin Muir, *The Ring* (with an unusual final pattern).

QUATRAIN

Definition: Any verse of four rhyming lines; the possible rhyme-schemes are: abab, abcb, aaaa, abba, aaab, aaba.

(*a*) 'Common Measure'—the C.M. of the hymn books. Lines alternating eight and six syllables, rhyming abab or abcb.
EXAMPLES: Coleridge, *The Ancient Mariner* (with variations), and many of the old ballads.

(*b*) 'Long Measure'—the L.M. of the hymn books. Quatrains with eight syllables in every line, rhyming abab or abcb.
EXAMPLES: A number of the ballads; Tennyson, *In Memoriam* (but rhyming abba).

(*c*) 'Short Measure'—the S.M. of the hymn books. Quatrains of 6.6.8 and 6 syllables, rhyming abab or abcb.

(*d*) The 'Omar Khayyam' quatrain—iambic pentameter rhyming aaba.
(*e*) The 'Gondibert' or 'Elegiac' stanza of Gray's *Elegy*, Sir William Davenant's *Gondibert*.

SONNET

Definition: A poem of fourteen iambic pentameter lines, with one of the following rhyme-schemes:
Shakespearian: abab cdcd efef gg.
Petrarchan or Italian: abba abba cde cde *or* abba abba ccd eed.
Spenserian: ababbcbccdcdee

There is usually a break in the sense between the octave (first eight lines) and sestet (last six lines) or, in the Shakespearian sonnet, the only break is sometimes before the final couplet.

EXAMPLES: The sixteenth century was the time when the sonnet, and the long sonnet sequence, enjoyed a vogue —almost an epidemic. Minor sonneteers can be tedious; but the age produced the sonnets of Shakespeare, Spenser, Sidney, Daniel, Drayton. The fashion ended, but the sonnet never died; see, e.g. the *Holy Sonnets* of Donne; E. B. Browning, *Sonnets from the Portuguese*; G. M. Hopkins, the sonnets in his collected poems; Peter Porter, *The Sanitized Sonnets*.

The TAILED SONNET surprises the reader by adding extra lines, e.g. Milton, *On the New Forcers of Conscience under the Long Parliament*; Hopkins, *Tom's Garland*. The sixteen-line poems of George Meredith's *Modern Love* may perhaps be seen as extended sonnets, though not the usual 'tailed' form.

In addition to the extended sonnet forms, G. M. Hopkins invented the *curtal sonnet*, of ten and a half lines; his *Pied*

Beauty is well known. This form has ten and a half lines, grouped in six and four with one short final line.

OTTAVA RIMA

Definition: Eight iambic pentameters rhyming abababcc.
EXAMPLES: Byron, *Don Juan, Beppo*; Keats, *Isabella*; Yeats, *The Municipal Gallery Revisited*.

SPENSERIAN STANZA

Definition: Eight iambic pentameters followed by one iambic hexameter (Alexandrine) and rhyming ababbcbcc. Probably the most ornate and splendid English verse-form to be found in narrative poems.
EXAMPLES: Spenser, *The Faerie Queene*; Byron, *Childe Harold's Pilgrimage*; Shelley, *The Revolt of Islam*; Keats, *The Eve of St Agnes*.

RHYME ROYAL

sometimes called *'Troilus' stanza* or *Chaucerian stanza*
Definition: Seven iambic pentameters rhyming ababbcc.
EXAMPLES: Chaucer, *Troilus and Criseyde, The Clerk's Tale*; Henryson, *The Taill of the Uponlandis Mous, and the Burges Mous* (and other fables); Shakespeare, *The Rape of Lucrece*; Auden, *Letter to Lord Byron*; Peter Levi, *Thoughts out of Doors*.

Certain forms more at home in France than in Britain need space out of proportion to their frequency or importance. However, for the reader they often have the charm of virtuosity; and for the apprentice poet they are excellent exercises.

BALLADE

Definition: A poem of three stanzas plus a shorter stanza called the *envoy*, all using two rhymes only. The metre may be iambic or anapaestic; the 28-line ballade rhymes ababbcbc, ababbcbc, ababbcbc, bcbc; the 35-line ballade rhymes ababbccdcd, ababbccdcd, ababbccdcd, ccdcd. The last line of each stanza and the envoy is the same. The envoy is normally addressed to someone, often an unidentified 'Prince'.

EXAMPLES: Chaucer, *Lak of Stedfastnesse*; Swinburne, *Ballade of the Hanged*; G. K. Chesterton, *A Ballade of Suicide, A Ballade of the First Rain*; Austin Dobson, *A Ballade to Queen Elizabeth, On a Fan that Belonged to the Marquise de Pompadour*; Michael Scot, *Ballade of the Cats of Bygone Time.* The French ballades of François Villon are much more impressive poems than any English ones.

The form has variants: some early writers used this two-rhyme technique, but with more verses and no envoy; the *double ballade* has six stanzas before the envoy; the *chant royal* has five stanzas rhyming ababccddede and an envoy rhyming ddede, still with the last line always repeated.

RONDEAU

Definition: A fifteen-line poem, usually but not invariably in iambic tetrameters, rhyming aabba aabR aabbaR, where R is a (non-rhyming) refrain that is also the first half of the first line.

EXAMPLES: Sir Thomas Wyatt, *'What, no perdy!'*; Austin Dobson, *In After Days*, Walter Crane, *A Seat for Three*; Charles Dent Bell, *Solemn Rondeau*.

There is also a *rondeau redoublé*, rhyming abab baba abab baba abab babaR, each line of the first quatrain being used in order as the final line of the four subsequent quatrains, and the first half of the opening line as the final refrain. The *rondeau of Villon* has twelve lines only, in the pattern abba abR abbaR.

RONDEL

Definition: A poem of thirteen, occasionally fourteen, lines, metre not prescribed, rhyming abba, abab, abbaa, with the seventh and eighth lines repeating the first two and the last line repeating the first. In the fourteen-line rondel the extra line repeats the second.
EXAMPLES: W. E. Henley, *'Beside the idle summer sea'*; Ezra Pound, *Dieu! qu'il a fait* (somewhat loose). Another version of rondel is Chaucer's *Merciles Beaute*, three rondels rhyming abb abab abbabb, where the first two lines are also the sixth and seventh, and the first three lines are also the last three. There is also a *rondelet*, rhyming abRabbR, the refrain being the first half of the first line.

ROUNDEL

Definition (when the term is not used as an alternative to *rondeau* or *rondel*): An eleven-line poem, metre not prescribed, rhyming abaR bab abaR, with the first part of the first line acting also as the refrain.
EXAMPLES: Swinburne, *'A roundel is wrought'*; *A Dialogue*, in

which an argument between Man and Death is worked out in a set of three roundels.

TRIOLET

Definition: An eight-line poem, metre not prescribed, rhyming abaaabab, with the fourth line repeating the first line and the last two lines repeating the first two lines.
EXAMPLES: Robert Bridges, *'All women born are so perverse . . .'* G. M. Hopkins, *'The child is father to the man . . .'*; Thomas Hardy, *At a Hasty Wedding*.

VILLANELLE

Definition: A poem of nineteen lines, metre not prescribed, using two rhymes only arranged in five sets of three and one quatrain; there is more than one possible order of rhymes, but the first line is repeated at the end of the second and fourth tercets and the third line at the end of the third and fifth; then the final quatrain ends with the first and third lines.

So repetitive a form can easily be trivial and dull; but it can also have a sinister tolling effect that well suggests circular or obsessive thinking, and has in our own day been revived for serious poetry.
EXAMPLES: Austin Dobson, *'When I saw you last, Rose . . .'*; W. W. Skeat's contemptuous *Villanelle* (It's all a trick, quite easy when you know it. . . .)[1]; William Empson, *Missing Dates*; Auden, *If I Could Tell You*; Dylan Thomas, *Do not go Gentle into that Good Night*; John Wain, *Villanelle for Harpo*

[1] To be found in Michael Roberts, *The Faber Book of Comic Verse*, 1942.

Marx; Keith Douglas, *Villanelle of Sunlight*. Forms probably influenced by the villanelle may be noticed more widely, e.g. Kingsley Amis, *The Voice of Authority*.

SESTINA

Definition: a poem of six six-line stanzas plus a three-line stanza, metre not prescribed, though very short lines are unlikely; instead of a rhyme-scheme, the final words of each line are repeated in a different order in each stanza; the final tercet may have three of these words, or even all six, with three placed in the middle of the lines. In the strictest form there is an exact prescribed order for the repetitions. The effect may perhaps be compared to change-ringing on bells.

Though the form is extremely difficult and artificial, it has been used for good serious poems.

EXAMPLES: William Drummond, two beautiful *Sextains* among his love sonnets and madrigals; Ezra Pound, *Sestina: Altaforte*; John Heath-Stubbs, *Sestina (A Consolation)*; Auden, *Have a Good Time*.

T. S. Eliot in *The Dry Salvages*, part ii, used a form derived from the sestina, but with a sequence of rhymes and no tercet.

Auden's *Kairos and Logos* achieves a poem of complex content and imagery in the form of a series of four sestinas.

POULTER'S MEASURE

Definition: Alternating iambic hexameters and seven-foot lines, used a good deal by minor poets of the sixteenth century. This form, which is inclined to drag, can be broken up into Short Measure.

EXAMPLES: Nicholas Grimald, *A Truelove*; Queen Elizabeth I, *That Daughter of Debate*; Fulke Greville, Lord Brooke, *Epitaph on Sir Philip Sidney*; Nicholas Breton, *Phyllis*. (All these will be found in the *Oxford Book of Sixteenth Century Verse*.)

ENGLISH HEXAMETERS

Are to be divided into two quite different forms:

(1) Definition: Iambic hexameters, rhymed or unrhymed.

EXAMPLES: Michael Drayton, *Poly-Olbion*; Browning, *Fifine at the Fair*; Bridges, *Testament of Beauty* (loose). This is not a common English form but is a perfectly possible one.

(2) An attempt at imitating in English the effect of Greek and Latin hexameters, the general effect of which is something like English dactyls. As it is difficult to write a poem of any length in English dactyls, and there are no quantities in English, the experiment is seldom fully successful.

EXAMPLES: Longfellow, *Evangeline*; A. H. Clough, *The Bothie of Tober-na-Vuolich* (one of the best English poems in this form, still worth reading).

During the sixteenth century the distrust of the vernacular as less dignified and durable than the classical languages led to a strong movement for the use of classical metres in English led by such people, more scholars than artists, as Gabriel Harvey. Sidney and other poets made attempts at writing English quantitative verse.

TAILED RHYME, TAIL-RHYME STANZA, RIME COUÉE

Definition: A stanza in which two or more lines are followed by a shorter line, then two or more longer lines again, then another shorter line, with the short lines rhyming.

Often applied to the 'romance-six' stanza of many old romances: two iambic tetrameters, one trimeter, two tetrameters, one trimeter, rhyming aabccb.

EXAMPLES: Chaucer, *Tale of Sir Thopas*, Wordsworth, *Ruth*.

Another tail-rhyme stanza is the form, going back as far as eleventh-century French, which Robert Burns handled brilliantly and made his own, rhyming aaabab.

EXAMPLES: Burns, *Holy Willie's Prayer, Death and Doctor Hornbook, To a Louse, Address to a Haggis, To a Mouse*.

There are many other possible 'tailed' forms, some with strict rhymes in all lines, some looser.

EXAMPLES: Michael Drayton, *Nymphidia*; Tennyson, *The Lady of Shalott*; Hardy, *A Trampwoman's Tragedy, Weathers*; Auden, *'You are the town and we are the clock'* (from *The Witnesses*); Vernon Scannell, *Remembrance Day*, and, with long and short lines rhyming together, *Those Childish Fears*.

SKELTONICS

Definition: Lines of irregular metre, mostly short, rhyming, but more or less capriciously. The effect will vary according to the exact style of rhyming and length of lines used.

EXAMPLES: John Skelton, *Philip Sparrow, The Tunning of Elinour Rumming, Colin Clout*; Browning, *Waring*; Coventry Patmore, *To the Body*; Edward Thomas, *Words*; Robert Graves, *In the Wilderness*; Hilaire Belloc, *Tarantella*; Christina Rossetti, *Eve*; F. W. Harvey, *Ducks*.

Oddly, there are no specific terms for any of the five and six line stanzas, though a five-line stanza may be called a *cinquain* and a six-line stanza a *sestet*. If we wish to describe any of the very numerous unnamed verse forms, we have to analyse them briefly, e.g.

> Since thou hast view'd some Gorgon, and art grown
> A solid stone:
> To bring again to softness thy hard heart
> Is past my art.
> Ice may relent to water in a thaw;
> But stone made flesh loves Chymistry ne're saw.
>
> HENRY KING

may be described as a verse of six iambic lines, a tetrameter followed by a dimeter twice, then two pentameters, rhyming aabbcc.

Free verse needs a small chapter to itself. Some other verse forms are mentioned in chapter XX.

XVI FREE VERSE

> Bear witness for me, whereso'er ye be,
> With what deep worship I have still adored
> The spirit of divinest Liberty.
>
> COLERIDGE: *France: An Ode*

Free verse is not a verse form in the usual sense. It is defined chiefly by negatives: it is a kind of poetry that has neither a regular pattern of rhymes, nor a recognizable traditional metre.

Two other negatives should be added. Free verse is not some glorious revolutionary emancipation of poetry, allowing sincerities never before possible. No free-verse poet yet has come anywhere near the scale, the range, the impression of free movement in a huge world of creative energy, of Shakespeare, Wordsworth, Byron, Browning or even, I think, Yeats. Free verse is also not just a contradiction in terms excusing sloppy incompetence or laziness; readers who think that resemble the art critics who thought Picasso invented new techniques because he could not draw, a calumny his early drawings refute.

The term *free verse* should not be applied to: unrhymed poetry that has a regular rhythm making a repetitive pattern —*blank* verse, the unrhymed iambic pentameters so widely and variously used in English poetry and drama; rhythms derived from the experience of classical metres, such as Campion's mainly trochaic:

> Rose-cheeked Laura, come;
> Sing thou smoothly with thy beauty's
> Silent music, either other
> Sweetly gracing.

—the trochaic tetrameters of Longfellow's *Hiawatha*, the (curtailed) dactylic metre of Arnold's *Rugby Chapel*; probably not even Sylvia Plath's *Mushrooms*, which can be heard as predominantly though not uninterruptedly trochaic; nor, properly, to forms such as the Japanese *haiku* which, though unrhymed and unmetrical, are delimited by strict definitions. We should be careful not to classify a poem as 'free verse' just because we have failed to identify its unusual formal repetitive pattern, or do not know a name for it.

Since real free verse, by definition, does not have a formal repetitive pattern, it is not easy to generalize about it; in a sense there are as many free-verse techniques as there are free-verse poets. However, a very loose and tentative distinction of a few categories may help the beginner.[1]

1 INCANTATORY—the kind of free verse which seems to lend itself to chanting or to solemn declamation; its patterns may be patterns chiefly of repetition; the lines are usually long; the subject is treated seriously, with something of a prophetic or exalted manner, possibly some hint of ritual, of liturgy. There are marked, but not metrical, rhythms—cadences of solemn oratory rather than tuneful stress patterns.

[1] The suggested categories are my own and should not be used in examinations as if they were critical terms in general acceptance.

Such verse we find in the Authorized Version of the *Psalms*, the *Song of Solomon*, much of *Isaiah* and *Job*; James Macpherson's (partly fake) 'translations' from Ossian; most of Blake's Prophetic Books; most of Walt Whitman's poems, such as *Song of Myself*; many of D. H. Lawrence's; T. S. Eliot's *The Hollow Men* (though here the lines are short) and *Ash Wednesday*; Hugh MacDiarmid's *Diamond Body* or *On a Raised Beach*; Theodore Roethke's *Meditations of an Old Woman*; Peter Redgrove's *The Case*.

2 IMAGISTIC A school of poets known as the Imagists, led mostly by Amy Lowell, flourished in Britain and America between 1909 and 1917 and published four anthologies, to which the chief contributors were Amy Lowell, D. H. Lawrence, F. S. Flint, Richard Aldington, H.D. (i.e. Hilda Doolittle) and the young Ezra Pound. This movement soon disintegrated, but left a noticeable residue of influence. Imagistic free verse presents sharp, clear images and aims at concentration as being 'the very essence of poetry'. This is largely a poetry of exact word-pictures, often of concrete things well observed, but also perhaps of emotions.

We find signs of imagistic methods not only in the group of poets mentioned above, but in many others, for example Charles Tomlinson in his *In Winter Woods*, or Alasdair Maclean in his *The Peaceable Kingdom*.

3 COLLOQUIAL One of the strongest motives for using free verse is that it can represent more or less realistically the cadences, with their hesitations, and the not obviously rhetorical tone, of everyday talk, with such things as anecdotes, small notings of life's ironies and perplexities, the everyday recitative of work, domestic routine, trivial emotion and fantasy, slight comment, scraps of observation, the details of our individual lives. Such a method may be a very good one for giving an instant impression of reality, sincerity, spontaneity. It remains poetry, not chopped prose, by startling but apt choice of words, elegant patterns other than metrical, subtle imagery, and so on; though the difference between colloquial free verse and lively prose can be very marginal.

We must remember that an apparently relaxed, colloquial poetry of the apparently trivial may be achieved by unobvious artistic self-discipline and may be resonant with implications about the majestic mystery of life. We all experience that huge mystery more continuously through our own poor silly little everyday selves than through our rare moments of high-voltage imaginative insight. We had better also remember that a poem that impresses us by its air of marvellous spontaneity may have cost the poet hours of careful working out just how to sound so spontaneous! Such is art.

Basil Bunting in *What the Chairman Told Tom* marvellously catches the tone and diction of a pompous, odious, individual philistine for our rueful amusement—but also says a good deal about the problems of the artist in society, including a hint that the matter is not simple black-and-white. D. J. Enright is a master of partly colloquial free verse: his *Paradise Illustrated* can be enjoyed at once on one level as a witty, intentionally 'tasteless', ingenious, deliciously entertaining burlesque of *Paradise Lost*, made more pointed by occasionally interpolating actual lines from Milton; but when we have laughed our fill, and re-read the poem more carefully, tears may follow as we take in some underlying implications about our human condition.

4 KALEIDOSCOPIC 'Cinematic' would be the better word, if certain vices of the film world had not already brought it into common critical use to rebuke melodrama, sentimentality or stereotyped situations. We readily accept, when watching a film, that, without verbal comment or explicit bridging, the camera shifts from, say, hero chained to rock beside a dried-up river-bed, to clock in his home . . . thermometer in shade . . . dog lapping water-bowl . . . smiling wife putting beer into refrigerator . . . smiling villain raising binoculars . . . view through binoculars of slumped hero . . . then of nearing vultures . . . thermometer (risen) . . . clock (moved on) . . . wife (anxious) . . . and so on. Messages are implied by images that keep changing, as in a shaken kaleidoscope.

It may be partly from experience of the cinema that some twentieth-century poets have developed a technique of moving from one evocative image or allusion to another, without an obvious logical or grammatical framework. If the technique works for a given reader (who has usually *worked* also, co-operating with the poet), the various images and allusions conjure up the right associations, the juxtaposition makes the intended impression and the poem is seen to have a meaningful structure.

Examples that have already won respect include T. S. Eliot's *The Waste Land*, the *Cantos* of Ezra Pound, David Jones's *The Anathemata* and Basil Bunting's *Briggflatts*. While no artistic dogma inexorably links this technique to free verse, it would hardly fit any traditional form. (Imagine Spenserian stanzas confining language so essentially elusive, fragmentary, indirect.)

Such poetry makes great demands on the reader's time, cultural resources and sensitive intelligence; so great, that it is unlikely ever to delight more than a smallish minority; and the question of how much the poet is entitled to demand of the reader has no simple answer. If we decide that such a poem is not for us, we still do better to trust the poet, who may have worked over it for years, weighing every word, than to trust the dismissive sneerer who after two minutes quotes some apparent incoherence and snorts about this modern nonsense.

5 PLAYFUL Relaxed, unpretentious free verse, redeemed from sloppiness by clever diction and shrewd observation, is useful nowadays for poetic fun, as in the (often rhyming, often eccentrically) humorous verse of Ogden Nash, or Don Marquis's *archy and mehitabel*; some little poems by D. J. Enright, Norman MacCaig or Roger McGough; Edwin Morgan's *The Starlings in George Square*; Norman Nicholson's *Boo to a Goose*; Anne Ridler's *Jane Wakeful*; Gavin Ewart's *Daddyo* and *Arithmetic*. The playful may, of course, often carry some hinted deeper meanings.

6 LOGODAEDALIAN ('showing inventive artifice in words', though in a broad sense this is what all poetry is doing) is the best term I can suggest for poetry in which the poet arranges words in unfamiliar structures, beyond ordinary syntax, perhaps employing unusual punctuation and typography, even inventing words. Such novelties often outrage narrow-minded readers; but the humility of intelligent attention often finds pleasure and point in the adventure.

Three of the best-known poets sometimes trying such methods are E. E. Cummings in such poems as *here's a little mouse) and*, *or i say no world*, or *spring! may*; George Macbeth in *Pavan for an Unborn Infanta* (which uses permutations of only two syllables, CHI and AN, as a poem about pandas), or his

'Chinese' poems such as *A Deposed General*; or Edwin Morgan in *Boats and Places, The Computer's First Christmas Card*, or *Bees' Nest*. Cummings, Macbeth and Morgan have all amply proved their craftsmanship in numerous poems nearer to the central traditions; but their most logodaedalian exercises are enjoyable, at the very least as verbal pastimes.

7 MIXED MODES The above classification is, like all classifications of works of art, inadequate; and a great many free verse poems mix two or more of the above modes. For instance, Eliot's *Journey of the Magi* is so moving partly because it mixes an incantatory tone with bits of the colloquial: these men are important, their purpose is religious; they are also real and very like ourselves, grousing a bit at the trials of travel. *The Waste Land* exemplifies at length such mixing and the poignant or shocking effects it can have. A long poem in free verse usually does some shifting from one mode to another; we may find examples in Alan Bold's *The Tomb of David Hume* (which also includes three sonnets, a few quatrains and a villanelle!) or Tony Connor's *The Memoirs of Uncle Harry*.

8 PLAIN LAZY We should always, in literary studies as in human relations, be slow to make harsh judgments and ready to believe that our own insensitivity may be a factor in our disapproval; but, now that educated readers accept free verse as legitimate, we do sometimes see 'poems' that are no more than jotted thoughts. The writer expects other people to think, and often himself honestly believes, that nowadays to write down something he thinks, feels, or observes, just as it comes, creates a poem. It may be, on a very small scale, by a fluke, once; but normally anything that deserves to be called a poem is the result of much self-discipline; whether or not the poet uses rhyme or metre, there will be some sort of organized structure, some originality of expression, something that has cost an effort.

Victorian magazines contain hundreds of sloppy little 'poems' with respectable metres and real rhymes and no merit whatsoever; plenty of rhyming rubbish was printed in the eighteenth century; bad 'free verse' is only a new variety of lazy pseudo-poetry; but it looks even easier to the person deficient in self-criticism to write 'poems' in 'free verse'.

Good free verse, however, is by no means a soft option. Just as a poor lyric may survive for decades if linked to a good tune, so a mediocre poem may lull the reader's critical faculty by a firm, hypnotic rhythm: we may think of Alfred Noyes's interminable invitation to come down to Kew in lilac time, or some of Tennyson's weaker poems, such as *The May Queen.* We may excuse a minor infelicity if it was forced on the poet by a very difficult verse form. It is a good deal harder to write some free verse that is unmistakably authentic original poetry than to write a drawing-room ballade that will serve its turn as a compliment.

Though free verse is characteristic of our present century, it should not be thought of as our principal technique. It is difficult to see how acceptable statistics could be compiled —who is to decide which poets deserve to be included in a survey?—but probably a majority of the reasonably good English poets of this century have used, for at least part of their work, traditional verse forms, or novel forms that do make regular repetitive patterns.

XVII THE CHOICE OF WORDS

Thy words are like a cloud of winged snakes.
SHELLEY: *Prometheus Unbound*

Poetry is made of words, and obviously the choice of words is important in poetry; indeed, in a sense it is the whole art of writing poetry. We have already considered the choice of words from the point of view of their accentuation (producing rhythm), their sound (producing onomatopoeic and rhyme effects) and their associative value; but a little attention ought also to be paid to the choice of words for their actual 'intellectual' meaning. This sounds so obvious as to be foolish, but inexperienced students of poetry sometimes forget all about it in the excitement of studying techniques of rhythm and pattern.

We may assume that the poet knows more or less what he wants to say before he sits down to write a poem. One does not usually sit down before a sheet of blank paper with a blank mind. An image has come into the poet's head; a rhythm is singing in the poet's ear; perhaps a logical sequence has already shaped itself and the choice of words will be dictated by these considerations. However, if we look at a manuscript left by any well-known poet we shall nearly always find that the poet has made many erasures and alterations before arriving at the final version. This process of polishing is very important. During the polishing, the poet is usually dealing with individual words; he may exclude a word because its sound echoes or clashes with the sound of another where such an effect is not wanted.

> And in his grave the weird worms squirm

would be a line of appalling badness; it would be some improvement to say:

> And in his grave the long worms creep.

The poet may find that in the excitement of composition he has wrenched an accent unnaturally or committed some inaccuracy of fact; he may become doubtful of the strict meaning of a word, or its accentuation, and need to check this in the dictionary; but most polishing is probably done in a search for the *mot juste*, the most exact and effective word possible in the context.

Unless the poet is aiming at some special sound effect of repetitive magic, he will usually try to convey his meaning in as few words as possible, a virtue which is equally applicable to good prose. The poets of the 1930s[1] who were so concise that their enemies described their work as 'telegraphese' were not merely being tiresome; aiming at crisp conciseness, they may have exceeded, but they were trying to do something entirely sensible and desirable, to concentrate as much meaning as possible into every line, as the Imagists tried, though in a different way. Most of us have met the temptation to pad a piece of written work to make it look more impressive, and learned that the result is as dreary

[1] Auden, Day Lewis, Spender.

as a pasty with too much pastry and too little meat. The poet may have an extra temptation to pad in order to fill out a metrical line. Any poet of integrity tries both to avoid redundant words, and to use not merely a word that will more or less do, but the exactly right word.

The words that can most easily be altered in polishing a poem are adjectives and adverbs. Let us first look at a few examples of brilliantly appropriate adjectives:

The *belching* whale
And *humming* water must o'erwhelm thy corpse,
Lying with *simple* shells!

SHAKESPEARE: *Pericles*

It might be argued that water does not hum; but anyone whose head has gone under the surface of the sea during a swim will recognize the sense-impression.

How shall your *houseless* heads and *unfed* sides,
Your *looped* and *windowed* raggedness, defend you
From seasons such as these?

SHAKESPEARE: *King Lear*

Dancing in the *chequered* shade.

MILTON: *L'Allegro*

And bid the *weltering* waves their *oozy* channel keep.

MILTON: *Nativity Ode*

A *winning* wave, deserving note,
In the *tempestuous* petticoat. . . .

HERRICK

Bubbling runnels joined the sound;

COLLINS

> Where rivulets dance their *wayward* round,
> And beauty born of *murmuring* sound
> Shall pass into her face.
>
> WORDSWORTH

> When I have fears that I may cease to be,
> Before my pen has gleaned my *teeming* brain,
> Before *high-piled* books, in charactery,
> Hold like *rich* garners the *full-ripened* grain. . . .
>
> KEATS

We have only to replace a few of these adjectives with others that do not spoil the metre, in order to appreciate the greater aptness of those the poets used:

> Dancing in the spotted shade. . . .

> A pretty wave, deserving note,
> In the tumultuous petticoat. . . .

> Streaming runnels joined the sound. . . .

In two of the above examples we have also brought in an excess of those annoying s's.

It has, however, been suggested that whereas an immature poet gains all his best effects of apt description from his adjectives, a mature great poet gains fewer effects from adjectives and more from verbs. There is an interesting example of how the importance of verbs increases in Wordsworth's *Prelude*; the 1805 version is the fresher and probably the more sincere, for the poet of 1850 had slid somewhat towards conventionality, a dangerous quality in poets; but the style has been improved in the later version. Often Wordsworth replaced a colourless 'was' or 'is' by some more definite verb:

1805. The sea was laughing at a distance. . . .
1850. The sea lay laughing at a distance.

Similarly in Wordsworth's *Michael* the first version:

Beside the brook
There is a straggling heap of unhewn stones!

The later version is:

Beside the brook
Appears a straggling heap of unhewn stones!

When Pope in his translation of the *Iliad* replaces

Destruction hovers o'er yon devoted wall

by

Destruction hangs o'er yon devoted wall

the reason is obvious. Here are some examples of very apt verbs from well-known poems:

Save where the beetle *wheels* his droning flight
GRAY: *Elegy*

Ride ten thousand daies and nights
Till age *snow* white hairs on thee;
DONNE

And the caked snow is *shuffled*
From the ploughboy's heavy shoon . . .
KEATS

Shine out, little head, *sunning* over with curls. . . .
TENNYSON

Ah Love! could thou and I with Fate *conspire*

To *grasp* this sorry Scheme of Things entire,
Would we not *shatter* it to bits, and then
Remould it nearer to the Heart's Desire!

FITZGERALD: *Rubaiyat of Omar Khayyam*

Where our sheep
Half asleep
Tinkle homeward through the twilight, *stray* or *stop*
As they *crop*—

BROWNING

How neatly 'tinkle' both suggests the sound, and, by telling us that the sheep are wearing bells, also suggests that the scene is exotic!

The chidden billow seems to *pelt* the clouds;

SHAKESPEARE: *Othello*

Ram thou thy fruitful tidings in mine ears . . .

SHAKESPEARE: *Antony and Cleopatra*

Why should I write this down, that's *riveted*,
Screw'd to my memory?

SHAKESPEARE: *Cymbeline*

Perhaps contemporary writers are more self-consciously concerned about the apt word than writers have ever been; this extreme self-consciousness often leads them into slight pedantry or what may look like misplaced cleverness; but more often it produces something refreshingly original that has arisen out of careful observation, alert imagination and well-stocked vocabulary. The last quality is a necessary one for a good poet; if he is to choose strictly accurate words, he must know the words first, just as all of us, if we are to avoid clichés in our prose writing, must be capable of putting together our own expressive phrases. Originality is one of the perennial delights of poetry; and one of the curious facts about it is that what seems most original is also often what is most true and exact. Perhaps the pleasurable surprise we receive whenever we notice a particularly apt word is an indictment of our general lack of precision in speech and writing!

XVIII TWO POEMS ANATOMIZED

Cut into small pieces.
Any Cookery book, *passim*.

Although I hope this book will not be used as a cram-book for examinees, since poetry is not a 'subject' to be 'crammed', but a great art to be loved, I have written it with one eye on examination candidates, so I am including a detailed discussion of two poems to show the kind of thing examiners expect. (I have marked thousands of examination papers!) The following simple examples of detailed criticism of poetry are, of course, themselves open to criticism; they are offered merely as an example of the kind of thing that can be said about a poem. There is no originality, as far as I know; brilliant original criticism of the standard of Johnson's *Preface to Shakespeare*, or Empson's *The Structure of Complex Words*, will always be rare, and the kind of person who is helped by this book is not likely to be able to write it.

Let us take, first of all, a simple poem on which, it may seem, very little can be said, Marlowe's *The Passionate Shepherd to his Love*, written about 1600. For ease of reference, we will have a copy with the lines numbered:

1 Come live with me and be my love,
2 And we will all the pleasures prove,
3 That hills and valleys, dales and fields,
4 And all the craggy mountains yields.

5 There we will sit upon the rocks
6 And see the shepherds feed their flocks,
7 By shallow rivers to whose falls
8 Melodious birds sing madrigals.

9 And I will make thee beds of roses
10 With a thousand fragrant posies,
11 A cap of flowers, and a kirtle
12 Embroidered all with leaves of myrtle.

13 A gown made of the finest wool
14 Which from our pretty lambs we pull;
15 Fair lined slippers for the cold
16 With buckles of the purest gold;

17 A belt of straw and ivy buds,
18 With coral clasps and amber studs:
19 And if these pleasures may thee move,
20 Come live with me and be my love.

21 The shepherd swains shall dance and sing
22 For thy delight each May morning:
23 If these delights thy mind may move,
24 Then live with me and be my love.

To write a useful criticism of this I must consider verse-form, sound-patterns, content, associations, use of repetition, logical sequence and anything else that is worthy of comment, ending with some general assessment.

Although Marlowe was a Londoner and in many ways

highly sophisticated, this poem praises the joys of country life. This country life, however, is ideal rather than real; it is a townsman's picture of life in the country. The birds, like educated Elizabethan youths, sing madrigals, which are rather beyond the limited intelligence of the average thrush or lark; beds of roses have no thorns or earwigs; and a shepherdess can afford coral, amber and gold, as well as having remarkably little to do. Moreover, wool is removed from lambs by the unkind and inappropriate process of pulling, instead of with shears. Thus the poem cannot be taken very seriously. It is an escapist poem, in the well-established pastoral tradition: sophisticated people fantasize about being innocent, simple shepherds and shepherdesses in idealized rural scenes.

As befits the artificiality of the theme, the rhythm is unadventurous, the metre conventional. Though the poem is printed as quatrains, it is really a set of twelve couplets, the rhyme-scheme being aa bb cc . . . ll. The metre is iambic tetrameter with very few variations; indeed, this poem, like Marlowe's dramatic verse, is so regular and so end-stopt as to be somewhat stiff and monotonous. Inversion of the first foot is to be found in line 5, inversion of the second foot in line 13 and a weak second foot in line 16; there is a weak third foot in lines 7, 11 and 15; the weak foot in line 7 finds compensation in the rather strong line 8. Feminine rhyme is a pleasant variant in the third verse. This sounds rather dull, but the conventionality of the rhythm is suited to the subject; a translation of the poem into free verse could be nothing but ironical.

By present-day English usage the word 'yields' with a decidedly plural subject is ungrammatical, but usage was less rigid in Marlowe's day; similarly the rhymes 'love–

prove' and 'sing-morning' are not very acceptable to a modern ear, but rules of pronunciation were more flexible in Marlowe's day, and a detailed knowledge of phonetic history would be necessary to comment on these apparently imperfect rhymes. In so conventional a piece they must be intended as full rhymes.

The repetition of 'Live with me and be my love' heightens the impression of persuasion. The passionate shepherd's wooing is sadly lacking in passion, his pleadings being all offers of material or at best aesthetic pleasures. The list of offered pleasures is, however, pictorial and attractive. It is these pictures and the associations clustering round them which give the poem its general appeal. The 'hills and valleys, dales and fields and all the craggy mountains' suggests a varied and extensive landscape; the 'rocks' so near to the 'craggy mountains' emphasize the romantic ruggedness of the scene, and the rivers and birds add music to visual beauty. (Mountain streams do indeed make a more musical noise than valley streams, one of the few realistic touches in the poem.) Then we leave the crags to lie upon beds of roses and play with flowers. The flowers are conventional—roses and myrtle,[1] both associated with young love, and vague 'fragrant posies', but the mention of flowers is almost always a successful evocation of beauty and freshness. The 'cap of flowers' fancy is not meaningless to people who have in childhood made cowslip balls or daisy chains; the 'pretty lambs' are a natural image of youth, innocence and simplicity. Everyone likes lambs. 'Slippers' are somehow more domestic and feminine than 'shoes', and have more associa-

[1] So conventional are the love-symbols of the poem that I feel it is to Marlowe's credit that he has chosen a less obvious rhyme than a 'faithful turtle'!

tions of affection and tenderness, perhaps because most of us have experience of a kind hand bringing our slippers for us at some time. The 'belt of straw and ivy buds with coral clasps and amber studs' is, if taken with flippant literalness, tasteless, semi-precious stones being a most unsuitable trimming for a belt of leaves and straw, though the latter are practicable materials for a shepherdess. In fact, however, by the combination Marlowe is suggesting the fusion of two worlds; we are to have both irresponsibility (the pastoral simplicity and childlike play of the rustic belt) and riches (coral and amber), just as we are to have a gown of natural wool and golden buckles. This seems to me to be the emotional key of the poem; Marlowe is implying something like: 'My dear, let us go and play at being shepherds and shepherdesses; we need not share their hardships; when we have made a rustic belt we can decorate it with the jewels we have brought from London.' This is a poem about the play of rich citizens who fancy some fresh air. They will, indeed, patronize the shepherds, encouraging them in their May-games, but watching, not taking part.

It is perhaps appropriate to the elegant atmosphere that the chief ornament of the poem should be alliteration, which is found in no fewer than thirteen lines out of the twenty-four. There are also a few pleasant internal echoes such as the l-sound in the first verse, generally a soft and soothing sound, and the interweaving of l- and s-sounds with pleasant onomatopoeic effect in the fourth couplet, where the sounds are appropriate to the rivers and birds.

This is not a profound or particularly sincere poem; if it is to be taken seriously, it earns Sir Walter Raleigh's dry retort beginning:

If all the world and love were young,
And truth in every shepherd's tongue,
These pretty pleasures might me move
To live with thee and be thy love.

But it must be accepted as a poem in the pastoral convention, of which it is a refined and pretty example.

The student will, I fear, notice in this little specimen of criticism a fault prevalent in all criticism, most of all in reviewing—a hint of patronage. If we are to judge something, we have to make a temporary and usually quite false assumption that we stand above it. This is not very good for the human soul, though if aesthetic studies are to exist at all we must sometimes take the risk.

Let us now analyse a more subtle and difficult poem, in which the verse form is rather more elaborate, the content more profound and the use of associations more delicate, so that a somewhat longer criticism will be possible. Here is James Shirley's famous *The glories of our blood and state*:

1 The glories of our blood and state
2 Are shadows, not substantial things;
3 There is no armour against Fate;
4 Death lays his icy hand on kings:
5 Sceptre and crown
6 Must tumble down,
7 And in the dust be equal made
8 With the poor crooked scythe and spade.

9 Some men with swords may reap the field,
10 And plant fresh laurels where they kill;
11 But their strong nerves at last must yield;
12 They tame but one another still:

13 Early or late,
14 They stoop to fate,
15 And must give up their murmuring breath,
16 When they, pale captives, creep to death.

17 The garlands wither on your brow,
18 Then boast no more your mighty deeds;
19 Upon Death's purple altar now
20 See where the victor-victim bleeds:
21 Your heads must come
22 To the cold tomb;
23 Only the actions of the just
24 Smell sweet and blossom in the dust.

As no one disputes the fact that great and obscure alike must die, the value of this poem is to be found in the rich associations. It is didactic in tone, but this richness prevents it being flat and dull as didactic poetry often is. Although it is on a solemn subject, the inevitability of death, 'the paths of glory lead but to the grave', some of the ambiguities are almost humorous, like Donne's holy puns. Though a minor poem, it is a mature one.

The form is fairly simple: an iambic tetrameter quatrain rhyming abab is followed by an iambic dimeter couplet and an iambic tetrameter couplet. The two dimeters lighten the lyric and make it natural that it should be set to music and sung; it is, indeed, a true lyric, for it comes from a play in which it was sung. The large number of long vowels would help the singer. The rhymes are all monosyllabic full rhymes and need no comment; there are no internal rhymes. There is considerable trochaic counterpoint, which saves the rhythm from being too ponderous: inversions of the first foot are found in lines 4, 5, 9, 11, 13, 20 and 23, with weak first feet in lines 3, 7, 8, 16, 19 and 22. In the tetrameter lines, inversion of the second foot is found in line 19, inversion of the third foot nowhere, but a weak second foot in lines 1 and 2, and a weak third foot in lines 3, 12, 17 and 23, a strong second foot in lines 8, 10, 11, 16, and a rather strong fourth foot in the very heavy line 11. In the dimeter lines of the poem inversions already mentioned lighten the poem more than those in the tetrameter lines, being proportionately more noticeable.

A paraphrase of the poem would suggest that the content, though hardly trivial, is so obvious as to be scarcely worth twenty-four lines of painstaking and musical verse: 'Earthly distinction is unreal, being ended by death, which is as inevitable for a king as for an agricultural labourer. Warriors may gain fame by killing, but are themselves overcome by death. Fame is transient, victors are victims, all are mortal; only good actions survive after death.' In fact, the poem says rather more than this.

The extremely concrete imagery strengthens the poem and helps to make it more than tedious moralizing on a platitude. Even rank becomes 'blood' (usually a disturbing word); there is no 'armour' to protect us from our fate and the hand of death is 'icy'—a real hand; regality is portrayed as 'sceptre and crown' and these representative objects do not 'fall' but, more brutally and in homely language, 'tumble', which suggests the weakness and helplessness of childhood. The poor man is not a vague 'shepherd swain' but is typified by his 'scythe and spade'; Fame is a laurel and a literal 'garland'; since the 'garland' is real it must soon 'wither'. The actions of the just are flowers that 'smell sweet'.

The altar of death is 'purple', catching up the colours of

both 'blood' and 'state', and the 'cold tomb' reminds us of the 'icy hand' of death. This 'catching up' of images, as a jewel at the throat may catch up the glitter of a shoe buckle, is one of the most artistic features of this poem. Sceptre, crown, scythe, spade, are laid equal in the dust; but it is also in the dust that the actions of the just blossom. The 'poor crooked scythe' leads on to those who, less harmlessly, 'reap' the field with swords—a truly horrible metaphor, if we visualize it at all clearly. I think it likely that Shirley takes advantage here of the association of the scythe with both Time and Death, and may possibly also be thinking of the scythes on the wheels of Ancient British chariots, which hideously 'reaped the field'. The laurels planted by warriors on the field manured with blood (I think we are meant to understand line 10 in this brutal way; blood is good manure for the laurels of military fame) catch up the garlands on the brows of conquerors and are contrasted with the flowers of the actions of the just; the flowers smell sweet; blood and laurels both have an unpleasant smell.

The actions of the just are presented as some loved, unobtrusive flower such as the violet. There is a subtle use of associations in the use of garlands and laurels as a symbol for the wrong kind of fame and the use of captives led to the altar as a symbol for death. For sacrificial victims are garlanded:

> To what green altar, O mysterious priest,
> Lead'st thou that heifer lowing to the skies,
> And all her silken flanks with garlands dressed?
>
> KEATS: *Ode on a Grecian Urn*

There is thus a hint that in acquiring laurels the warriors are really preparing themselves for the sacrificial altar. 'Purple', too, is associated with royal and triumphal robes as well as with blood; the sound-echo in 'victor-victim' and even the brilliant use of 'blood' in the first line all help to build us a half-conscious acceptance of an actual equating of fame with death. It is a wonderful piece of virtuosity in the handling of associations and ambiguous words. We may also be meant to think of the wreaths used at funerals.

This seems at first sight a rather ordinary poem, and we wonder why it moves and haunts us until we begin to analyse these cross-currents.

XIX HOW NOT TO APPROACH POETRY

Polonius: This is too long.
Hamlet: It shall to the barber's, with your beard. Prithee, say on; he's for a jig, or a tale of bawdry, or he sleeps.

SHAKESPEARE: *Hamlet*

The practice of setting pieces of poetry to be commented upon in an examination ought to be a good test of sensitivity, intelligence and articulateness; unfortunately, it can also be a test of mere glibness. It is easy to pick up a critical vocabulary and a few clichés of criticism. It is easy to pretend that we like something when we are not really interested; it is easy to pretend we disapprove of something we like if we think this is what is expected of us; and it is sometimes easier to write fluently about something in which we are not interested than about something we really love and revere. It is easy to count syllables and gain a few marks by being able to do arithmetic. Even more disastrously easy is the habit of using a few words like 'effective', 'beautiful' and 'expressive' and a few simple technical terms like 'figurative' and 'personification' without knowing anything worth knowing about poetry.

Poetry is now so little read that many people meet it only at school, and study it seriously only with a view to examinations. If the teaching happens to be uninspired —and it is exceedingly difficult to teach poetry well to pupils from homes in which poetry has no place—it may merely replace an ignorant indifference with a positive dislike. And the ambitious pupil, who wants examination certificates, may parrot opinions or embark prematurely on reluctant analysis without genuine intellectual curiosity.

Before the novel became our principal form of reading for pleasure, such people as today welcome new novels eagerly welcomed new narrative poems by Scott or Byron. Commercially successful poetry is today very rare. Other reasons for the diminished public for poetry probably include: the trivializing influence of many popular newspapers and magazines; the development, with radio and still more with television, of instantly accessible, undemanding and rather addictive entertainment in most homes; and, because so many of us have the bad habit of keeping radio or television switched on in the background when we are *not* enjoying it, a deterioration in our powers of attentive listening; the rarity of speech good enough to fit us for reading poetry aloud, so as to give pleasure, even in the family circle;[1] and a

[1] Clear speech, like legible handwriting, is a kindness to everyone else; good recitation and acting are worthwhile pursuits. We can improve our speech, as Eliza Doolittle did, and without anyone as formidable as Higgins. However, since some poor teachers of 'elocution' can teach unattractive affectations, anyone seeking coaching in speech should check a teacher's qualifications. Reputable training bodies include: London College of Music, Guildhall School of Music and Drama, Trinity College of Music, Royal Scottish Academy of Music and Drama, Royal Academy of Dramatic Art, Central School of Speech and Drama, Royal Academy of Music; and some universities and colleges of education have courses in Speech and Drama.

distrust of the arts which easily gets mixed up with those miserably *un*-progressive concepts of democracy that proscribe any real intellectual pursuits as 'elitism', instead of wanting the richest possible intellectual life to be available to every citizen.

There are further obstacles. Much old poetry is genuinely somewhat difficult if we do not have help with obsolete words and forgotten allusions. Bookshops and public libraries often have very little poetry on display, and new volumes of poetry are not much advertised. Then, too, many good poets of our own epoch have written difficult, even cryptic, poetry, aimed at a minority; though sometimes a well-publicized, easier poet such as Betjeman collects a good readership, many people may be put off poetry by, say, Eliot and Pound, when they could enjoy work that is less cryptic but in fact very good, such as the poetry of Philip Larkin, Vernon Scannell, Robin Skelton, Anne Ridler, Kathleen Raine, Louis MacNeice—many more names could be added. Or one clotted poem by George Barker, one trickily allusive poem by Auden, may put off the reader who would greatly enjoy at least half the poems of Auden, all the easier work of Barker.

Some people may also still be affected by the odd myth that poets and poetry are sentimental, soppy, useless, though there is no shortage of poets admirable for courage and enterprise, and good poetry tends to be very tough stuff in its self-discipline and intellectual and emotional honesty.

At all events, with one thing or another many people come to examination work on poetry with very little experience of poetry reading, perhaps no experience of real joy in poetry; and this can lead to some very unreal methods of study.

I cannot suggest how this can be entirely avoided; if we are to have the criticism of poetry on examination papers, some degree of 'cramming' is sure to happen; if we leave poetry out of 'set books' and off examination papers, poetry will probably be read less rather than more; and the study of a subject for an examination does not automatically spoil it for us; it may even bring us our first really pleasurable insights. The reader may, however, be warned of the dangers of three regrettable ways to approach poetry.

The first may be called *Pleasing-the-Examiners*, or, more generally, *Insincere Conformity*. In an authoritarian classroom, or even home, a youngster may find it prudent to accept dictated opinions and be ruefully cynical about temporary expediency. (I was interested to find, as an adult, the very book from which a teacher had literally dictated our notes, our opinions on poets to be memorized.) It may be even more desperately expedient to conceal appreciation of poetry from the bully in the cloakroom than to fake it for the well-meaning stereotyper in the classroom. Probably most of us have at some time to swallow some minor shames of this kind;[1] we can be thankful that in Britain they are occasional and particular, when totalitarian regimes enforce whole systems of prescribed opinions.

Within the confines of the authoritarian community, it may be sensible to conform, though, if hypocrisies are forced upon us, it is important to remember, secretly, what

[1] As a very young teacher I was once cornered into apologizing to a senior for *understanding* a poem by Louis MacNeice. It was evidently unprofessional to understand any of that nasty modern poetry, already ruled to be incomprehensible. No, I wasn't understanding it rudely or even loudly.

we are conceding, and why. External examiners, not trying to cope with thirty people at once, may be more friendly towards enquiring minds, originality and answers that are not just rehashes of classroom notes, than candidates suppose. If you had just waded through twenty-nine essays almost as similar as twenty-nine frozen shepherd's pies, wouldn't you be ready to welcome a thirtieth essay with a somewhat different flavour?

Taste in poetry must be in part subjective. Preference as between, say, Wordsworth and Pope; Byron and Shelley; Vernon Scannell and Anne Sexton—depends to a considerable extent on personal temperament. Immature taste is no disgrace in immature people; taste should through life change, mature, acquire more breadth and more complex nuances.

What we need to do, in worthwhile discussion of poetry, and in examinations, is to defend our current taste with reasonable evidence; not to gush, 'Isn't it lovely!' nor to snap, 'That's a load of old rubbish!' but to analyse the poem closely enough to identify some merits in it or to expose its real falsity.

A room full of desks, with a clock to glance at anxiously, more questions to answer, and an invigilator well supplied with extra paper, string, sealing-wax, lists of candidates, a glare for noises and water for faints, is not the ideal environment for sincere close study of poetry. However, from analysis as practised for examinations we at least learn something about poetic techniques, just as by dissecting a rabbit we learn a lot about the marvels of anatomy, without necessarily improving our relationships with animals.

Ideally, we should read poetry because we want to—because it gives us pleasure, has something to say to our situation, expands our consciousness; we should relax and let art happen to us before we jump up to say something about it. It is tragic when people dislike poetry because it was forced upon them clumsily. On the other hand, poetry is one of many delightful, interesting things we might not know about if we were not at some time told to look.

To an alert-minded lover of poetry a poem is not spoiled by being analysed; it becomes richer and more fascinating. It is perhaps unfortunate that the age at which we take important formal examinations is generally that during which our emotional and aesthetic susceptibilities are just developing, often with pain and uncertainties. Examination work can, with good teaching, help development, but can sometimes hinder it. However, it is never too late to develop the capacity to enjoy poetry or any other art. The now-famous American painter known as 'Grandma Moses' began painting when over seventy. My father, about six weeks before he died at the age of fifty-seven, suddenly had a new burst of aesthetic experience and 'discovered' contemporary poetry with immense enthusiasm and intelligence, after sneering at it for years.[1]

The second unlucky approach may be called the attitude of *Be Nothing if not Critical*. This is caused in part by the fact that the word *criticism*, which in literary contexts means the assessment of literature, in everyday contexts means only finding fault. Some teachers, trying to counter the fault-finding associations of the word *criticism*, make the association even stronger by speaking of *criticism and appreciation*. The really able critic is as often someone who can show us

[1] The poet who finally broke through his resistance was Anne Ridler.

good where we did not see it before, as the fault-finder, and is a much pleasanter person.

A totally uncritical response to poetry (or paintings, or meals, or football matches, or television) is fatuous: we can hardly enjoy the good intensely if we cannot perceive differences between the good (of its own kind) and the mediocre or bad. We should, however, be a bit cautious in finding fault. Good medicine for a too carping reader is to try to write a better poem, of such a kind, on such a scale, and in such a form that comparison is fair.

A reader, often though by no means exclusively the immature or inexperienced reader, may pounce with eager censure—because he has missed the point of the poem, of the metaphor or other detail of expression; because his concepts about, say, scansion are ignorantly narrow; because the experience of the poet is too far outside his own; because the technique is one he is not used to; because he has had an overdose of that particular technique; because he wants to seem clever, to place himself as superior to the poet (usually as aspiration downright comic); because he has the idea that a sophisticated, tasteful, discriminating person likes as few things as possible (almost as if a healthy stomach were the one sickened by nearly all foods); even because he does not like to hear anyone praised (a common manifestation of enviousness) or because a disliked teacher likes the poem.

Insincere conformity may in fact concur with sensible judgments; the over-critical approach demands at least a modicum of intelligence; another mistaken approach is that of *Total-Irrelevance*.

I once heard a professional teacher of English dismiss a new volume by Edith Sitwell as inevitably worthless, because, 'You know, I did once go to hear her read; and what she seemed most interested in was an enormous ring she was wearing.' Edith Sitwell's poetry is not everyone's cup of tea—and never aimed at being anything as banal as a cup of tea—but a trivial, ungenerous irritability over what, if true, may have been shyness and can have been nothing worse than minor vanity had nothing to do with the quality of the poetry. I have heard a sensitive, subtle poet dismissed as worthless because he was divorced; Auden and Spender, because they were not in the armed forces during the Second World War;[1] reactions to Byron's poetry have often been distorted by attitudes to his not irreproachable love-life; Rupert Brooke or Keats have been glamorized by early death . . . or someone may dislike *Horses on the Camargue* 'because I am afraid of horses'; *Dover Beach* because 'I once spent a horrible night in a Dover guest-house'; or *My Last Duchess* because 'I am against all class distinction'.

The beginning of all intelligent discussion of poetry is to focus attention on *the poem*, to consider what the author, in this particular work, is doing with words.

Our responses to poetry, as to many other things, are affected by our human tendency to unhappy relations between age-groups, nowadays called 'the generation gap'; and this is complicated by our tendency to turn against the tastes of our own childhood and adolescence, not only because our tastes do mature, but in order to convince ourselves that we are grown-up.

We must indeed follow Blake's advice to 'drive your cart and your plough over the bones of the dead', insist on our

[1] It has only recently become public knowledge that Auden was medically unfit for service; Spender could have been excused on medical grounds, but insisted on joining the Fire Service in London, hardly the most obvious way to keep out of danger.

right to make our own independent judgments, if we are ever to reach the higher level of maturity from which we are able also to see something of a previous generation's point of view. It is often the younger minds that respond most readily to new styles in poetry, and that find the content most relevant to their experience, though an immature mind can be as inelastic from insufficient stretching as an ageing mind from shrinkage. During our emancipation period we are not pleasant to live with, and we are often thinking of the effect of what we are saying, rather than its truth. When I was about seventeen my father was very fond of using Milton as a stick with which to beat the moderns whom I had already learned to love; I am very glad to say that I vividly remember shouting abuse of Milton at my father, weeping with fury. I am certain that I was right to go my own way; we learn far more by insisting on our freedom than by sitting meekly at someone's feet; the brutal and painful break has to be made. But I do not delude myself that I was lovable at the time; once I was free, I learned to love Milton also, and to go on abusing him when I had won my freedom would have been merely silly. Some people never get beyond this first stage of healthy rebellion.

We can be as inflexible about poetry of the past as about innovations! If we do not like an old poem at first sight, we may need to see it in its historical setting.

To sum up, any right approach to poetry will be very like any right approach to personal relationships, and not altogether easy, because we have somehow to push the bulging, intrusive, arrogant self into its proper place, and try above all to listen with genuine attention to the alien voice; not, first of all, to criticize, nor to relate to our own situation, nor even to paraphrase, but simply and courteously *to try to hear what the poet is trying to say*. It is foolish to expect every writer of every period to take for granted the same values as ourselves; in another hundred or even twenty years the accepted values will have undergone another change and our own writers will need to be seen in their historical setting to be fully appreciated. Though it is possible to enjoy a great deal of poetry without understanding either the history of poetry or the rudiments of national history, these studies help us a great deal by enriching our appreciation of allusions and emotions no longer current.

XX SOME TWENTIETH-CENTURY TECHNIQUES

> The old order changeth, yielding place to new,
> And God fulfils himself in many ways,
> Lest one good custom should corrupt the world.
>
> TENNYSON: *Morte D'Arthur*

This book is not a history of English poetry and cannot claim to dissect all the possible poetic anatomies of our experimental epoch; but, over a quarter of a century since the first edition, certain developments should be mentioned.

For several centuries English prosody has been dominated by the *accentual-syllabic* system, which gives us *feet*; the poet arranged *stresses*, or *accents*, at regular intervals, in lines consisting of regular numbers of syllables; the usual alternative was quantitative verse imitative of Greek or Latin prosody, which does not fit English comfortably.

We now find also in English both purely *accentual* and purely *syllabic* verse; both provide firm, disciplining frameworks, but, like snakes, the lines can move gracefully without feet.

Accentual verse is not an innovation, but goes right back

to Old English poetry such as *Beowulf*. There are, in each line, so many stressed syllables—usually four; but the number of unstressed syllables accompanying them is not fixed. Usually there is a pause *(caesura)* near the middle of the line, and two stresses are heard on either side of the caesura. Old English used patterns of alliteration to strengthen the rhythm, and modern poets, sometimes imitate this:

/ / / /
As *o*ne who *w*anders into old *w*orkings ('one' begins with the sound of w)
/ / / /
*D*azed by the noon*d*ay, *d*esiring coolness, (uncertain if a main stress is on 'barred', 'fall' or 'face')
/ / / / /
Has *f*ound retreat barred by *f*all of rock*f*ace;
/ / /
*G*ropes through *g*alleries where *g*ranite

/
bruises
/ / / /
Taut *p*alm and *p*anic *p*atters close at heel;

C. DAY LEWIS, *From Feathers to Iron*

A rather looser accentual verse, without such strong alliterative pattern:

/ / / /
They attend all the lectures on Post-War Problems,
/ / / /
For they do mind, they honestly want to help; yet,
/ / / /
As they notice the earth in their morning papers,

/ / / /
What sense do they make of its folly and horror, . . .
W. H. AUDEN, *A Healthy Spot*

/ / / /
Because it's wet, the afternoon is quiet.
/ / / /
Children pacified with sweets inside
/ / / /
Their small houses, stroke travelling cats (another reader might prefer to stress 'trav')
/ / /
From the kingdom of dustbins and warm
/
smells.
DOUGLAS DUNN, *Young Women in Rollers*

Such lines do not have the feet we are used to; but we can hear a regular throb, some kind of rhythm, under the meaning.

Lines with different numbers of stressed syllables can be arranged in stanzas:

/ / /
A leaf's otherness,
/ / / / /
The whaled monstered sea-bottom, eagled peaks
/ / / /
And stars that hang over hurtling endlessness,
/ / /
With manslaughtering shocks
TED HUGHES, *Egg-Head*

Ted Hughes's nine-stanza poem keeps up an almost completely regular pattern of three, five, four and three stressed syllables.

Modern accentual rhythm owes something to the 'sprung rhythm' of Gerard Manley Hopkins; he died in 1889, but his poems exploded like a delayed-action bomb into 1918. Hopkins's prosody, when not orthodox, as it sometimes was, has probably remained unique: his strange obsessive rhythms seem forced along by pressures of controlled emotion, giving impressions quite different from the sober, understated rhythms of poets such as Douglas Dunn.

According to Hopkins himself, 'Sprung Rhythm . . . is measured by feet of from one to four syllables, regularly, and for particular effects any number of weak or slack syllables may be used. It has one stress, which falls on the only syllable, if there is only one, or, if there are more, then scanning as above, on the first, and so gives rise to four sorts of feet, a monosyllable and the so called accentual Trochee, Dactyl, and the First Paeon.'[1] In Hopkins's unique scansion lines could be 'rove over', i.e. a 'foot' could extend into the next line. What I hear as the likely scansion of the lines below is not certainly in every detail what Hopkins intended, but gives some idea of his method:

/   /   /
Loathed for a | love men | knew in them, | dactyl, trochee, dactyl

/   /   /
Banned by the | land of their | birth.   dactyl, dactyl, monosyllable

[1] *Paeon*, in classical prosody, a four-syllable foot with one long syllable and three shorts; of the four possible arrangements, the First Paeon is thus: - ᴗ ᴗ ᴗ ; in English non-quantitative scansion, / . . ., e.g. *maximally*.

Rhine re | fused them. | Thames would | ruin them; |	trochee, trochee, trochee, dactyl
Surf, | snow, | river and | earth |	Monosyllable, monosyllable, dactyl, monosyllable
Gnashed: but | thou art a | bove, thou O | rion of | light	trochee, dactyl, dactyl, dactyl, ?monosyllable
Thy un | chancelling | poising | palms were | weighing the | worth,	?trochee, dactyl, trochee, trochee, dactyl, ?monosyllable.
Thou | martyr- | master: in | thy | sight |	?monosyllable, trochee, dactyl, monosyllable, monosyllable
Storm flakes were | scroll-leaved | flowers, | lily | showers— sweet | heaven was a | strew in them.	dactyl, trochee, trochee, trochee, dactyl, paeon, dactyl

The Wreck of the Deutschland

If Hopkins did not intend such an affirmative emphasis on 'Thy' and 'Thou' at the beginnings of the sixth and seventh lines, then we have a rove-over dactyl joining the fifth and sixth and a rove-over trochee joining the sixth and seventh.

Most modern accentual verse is much less startling than that of Hopkins, though the poets would probably seldom claim to be working with 'feet' as Hopkins still did; their rhythms are nearer to those of everyday speech. A minor but interesting poet the reader may like to compare with Hopkins in his prosody is W. R. Rodgers. Sparks of Hopkins's influence crackle in the lines of many successors —early Day Lewis, MacNeice, Spender, Dylan Thomas,

George Barker, for instance; but no one 'Came equipped, deadly-electric' with his strange lightning. One merely technical reason for the difference between Hopkins's Sprung Rhythm and the stress-counting of the other poets quoted is of course Hopkins's rule that the stress was always on the *first* syllable of a group.

Any counting of stressed syllables gives a pattern, a restriction; if versifiers do not have personal voices in addition to definable patterns, they are not poets. We may compare the blank verse of *The Tempest, Paradise Lost, The Prelude* and *Andrea del Sarto*—all iambic pentameters, all differentiated beyond any possibility of mistaken identity.

The principle of *syllabic verse* sounds like a soft option until we try it, when we are likely to realize that this too provides a strict, disciplining framework for the poem. The poet just keeps the same number of syllables in each line, or arranges stanzas in which there is the same number in each first, second, third line and so on. In practice, there may often be some hint of a stress pattern somewhere; and there is no reason why syllabic verse should not rhyme if the poet so wishes.

Rhyme has no significance in Japanese poetic technique, because so many Japanese words rhyme; and an interest in Japanese poetry in this century has been one of the influences on the development of modern English syllabics. The Japanese forms best known in the West are the *haiku*, a three-line lyric of five, seven and five syllables, and the *tanka*, a five-line lyric of five, seven, five, seven and seven syllables.

While many short, delicate poems, especially Imagist poems, suggest to an English reader something of the flavour of a translated Japanese lyric, the genuine English *haiku* or *tanka* remains very rare. The forms may, however, have contributed to one important novelty in English versification, which I will call *the prosody of the odd numbers*.

Since the iambic foot predominates so overwhelmingly in traditional English verse, most lines have had ten, twelve or eight syllables, or, much less commonly, some other even number. Trochaic lines are also even-numbered; even anapaests and dactyls will provide sixes or twelves at least as often as threes or nines in their infrequent appearances.

Poets writing syllabic verse have often tried the different music of lines of five, seven, nine, eleven and thirteen syllables; and this may be one of the most valuable functions of syllabic verse. George Macbeth's *A True Story* keeps strictly to a stanza of 9, 9, 9 and 7 syllables; Thom Gunn's *Considering the Snail* catches a strange new music—

> The snail pushes through a green
> night, for the grass is heavy . . .

with very regular seven-syllable lines.

A mixture of odd and even numbers of syllables can be startling, as in Marianne Moore's *The Fish*:

> Wade
> through black jade
> of the crow-blue mussel shells, one
> keeps
> adjusting the ash heaps;
> opening and shutting itself like
>
> an
> injured fan.

(Eight six-line stanzas keep this 1, 3, 8, 1, 6, 8 pattern.)

Auden, a virtuoso in syllabic verse as in many other techniques, used syllabic stanzas sometimes less strict than those already quoted, though they satisfy the ear; for instance, *At the Grave of Henry James* mixes long and short lines, 11/12, 11/12, 7/8, 14/15, 13/14, 7/8. (The complexity of both the form and the diction in this poem beautifully fits its subject.) *Hands* gives an impression of great regularity and control with its lightly varied pattern of, basically, 11, 9, 7, 6, 9, 6. Odd-number lines, 5, 7, 5, 5, 7, 5, give an unusual music to *The Art of Healing*:

> Most patients believe
> dying is something they do,
> not their physician,
> that white-coated sage,
> never to be imagined
> naked or married.

And, though he allowed himself some licences, Auden in his tribute to the outstanding pioneer poet of syllabics, *A Mosaic for Marianne Moore*, arrayed beautifully allusive compliments in a rigorously strict pattern of 12, 7, 12, 12, 5. (Anyone who thinks that easy should try it!)

George Macbeth has tried another kind of syllabic verse: his *Fourteen Ways of Touching the Peter* consists of fourteen splendidly accurate images of handling a cat, each using fourteen words. The exact arrangement of each group of fourteen fits the sensation, e.g.

> You can touch
> his

feet, only
if
he is relaxed.
He
doesn't like it.

Read with the appropriate tiny pauses, this gives just the right tentativeness and jerkiness of trying to touch a sleepy but suspicious cat's paws.

Ignorant or arrogant readers—and the words are often near synonyms—often reject good poems because they 'do not scan'. The poem may be good free verse, but if it seems to have some kind of repeating pattern, like, say, Dylan Thomas's *Poem in October* or Auden's *Fairground* or Marianne Moore's *His Shield*, we should, instead of pulling faces, try to spot the rules by which this particular game is being played. Any art is practised by independent individuals; at the same time, the beauty of any art arises partly from the wrestle with difficulty.

I remember a bit of pure joy with a group of students who, learning the rudiments of prosody, were testing various poems and themselves. Someone fished out Robert Graves's *Welsh Incident* and asked how to scan that. Well, yes, some iambics . . . but not regular . . . certainly not trochees, anapaests, dactyls . . . Accentual, perhaps? fours, fives? surely, if so, very wobbly, and Graves's austere craftsmanship is manifest in numerous other poems. Syllabic? line lengths range from eight to twelve syllables, not in a repeating pattern.

We were all perplexed. Then I tried reading the poem aloud in a dramatic style, and we burst out laughing; in this one poem Graves has done a brilliant humorous imitation of

Welshmen speaking English as they sound to an Englishman; and that is in fact here his rhythm!

Successful traditional techniques can be continued, can even be resurrected, if the new practitioner has the creative vitality to refresh them: Auden wrote sonnets, quantitative verse, alliterative verse, ballad quatrains, tail-rhyme stanzas, sestinas. . . . Poetry also needs new techniques if it is not to flop into decadent imitativeness. In looking at prosody, or any other aspect, we should try both to respect a good past and to be receptive towards explorations.

Probably the most freakish field of poetic exploration in the present century has so far been *Concrete Poetry*, developed in an international movement ranging over Europe, Turkey, the United States, Brazil and Japan. This may be seen as having developed out of the very ancient tradition of 'shaped poems' or 'pattern poetry' Edwin Morgan, a fine and versatile poet for whom concrete poetry is only one of several explorations, has a pomander-shaped poem in which the 'contents', normal words arranged in a kind of verbal pot-pourri, suggest the fragrant richness of life; and a poem about the great engineer Isambard Kingdom Brunel in the shape of a massive bridge, also suggesting a big metal bolt; these can be accepted as poems in the usual sense. When he creates his *Chaffinch Map of Scotland*, a map of Scotland made from local words for the chaffinch, or *French Persian Cats Having a Ball*, in which various permutations of *chat, shah* and *cha-cha* are so arranged as to suggest ballroom movement, or *Orgy*, in which 528 equidistant letters plus thirty asterisks produce an image of a hungry and finally sated anteater by permutations, possibly giving some sense of the non-logical mental experience of an animal, Morgan shows wit, ingenuity and charm, but whether these delightful games are poetry is open to question. *Orgy* can be read aloud, even amusingly; the other two need to be visual experiences.

Purists in the concrete-poetry movement, however, would say that Edwin Morgan's poems have too much verbal meaning to be fully 'concrete'.

Many poets use bits of typographical effect; for centuries poets have occasionally used italics for emphasis; Adrian Mitchell uses capitals and once uses letters going downwards to spell 'downstairs'; Roger McGough sometimes jumps words about the page for special effects; E. E. Cummings splits words, arranges them oddly and uses special styles of punctuation. Here is a verse that, for fun, uses typographical extras to emphasize its simple differentiations of character, perhaps in the office or on a committee:

e
n o r t
Steve is almost i c h en .
David talks *Good Sense.*
Jane is often v e r y v a g u e
Lucy, **VERY DENSE.**
Catty Cora's fffffull of sss*spite*,

O
Dick is rather D
D.

a l
n e
Liz is quite an G , but
Alan thinks he's **GOD.**

This, however, makes sense when just read aloud, without the visual jokes. If I wish to let off steam about a tiresome person who scatters trouble and irritation all around, and, instead of assembling metaphors, perhaps of itches and aches, a swarm of midges, an infection, radioactive fallout, etc., I express my opinion thus:

BOILING OVER

fuss uss fuss fuss fuss fuss
suss uss   fuss fuss fuss fuss
us fff uss fuss   fuss fuss
fuss   fuss fuss fuss
sssssssssss   fusspot potfuss fatpuss puspot fusspot fusspot pottyfusser
fizz fuss suss us   potfuss fusspot fizzpit pussfit fusspot fusspot pettyfuss
fuss
sssss fffff uuuussss   fusspot potfuss notpass fussfuss
spillfuss splash   fishpat fusspot fastvex potfuss
potty fuss fuss   fussnit pushpuss fussnurse suss
fuss fuss sssuss   fussynose nurseynose pussyfuss
hissfuss missfuss   sussfix fusspot fusspetty potty
thisfuss fizzfuss   usspusher pushpetty pussnos
fussmess misfuss   sspot fusspot fusspot pott
fussfall fussfail   past fussfast fussfizz f
fuss ss sss sss ssss   fusspit fusspatte
ssss sssss ssssssss
sssssssssssssssssssss
sssssssssssssssssssss
sssssssssssssssssssss
ssssssssssssssssssssss
ssssssssssssssssssssss
ssssssssssssssssssssss
ssssssssssssssssssssss
M E S S Y M E S S

this cannot be read aloud in full. I hope it does convey to someone else the idea that an unpleasant fusspot is 'like' a saucepan (pot) full of fuss, which boils over and makes a mess, like a pan of milk. The trick with words and letters is meaningful and may be amusing; but I doubt whether any bit of skill shown in it really comes in the field of poetry or even verse.

Concrete Poetry is seen rather than read. Words, mixed together, repeated, arranged in permutations, dislocated, suggest various relationships, resemblances, possibilities. Sometimes words are broken up and the letters distributed in patterns that, again, suggest, or are meant to suggest, various experiences of the concepts. Words or letters may be arranged in patterns, even in pictures. Ian Hamilton Finley wrote an appealing poem that meanders on the page like a stream, full mostly of murmuring *m*'s in many different founts[1] and *x*'s for windmills, or kisses, in which we can find the statement, 'this is the little burn that plays its mouth-organ by the m mm mmm mMm mill.' The total image is much more than the rational statement. Mathias Goeritz (born in Danzig, living in Mexico) repeated and repeated the word *oro*, 'Gold', in a series of rather beautiful square patterns that suggest wrought metal grilles suitable for a palace or shrine. The Czech Ladislav Novák printed GL RIA with the missing O set far above like the sun shining down (or a hovering halo?).

In America, Mary Ellen Solt created a series, *Flowers in Concrete*, in which flower names are disintegrated and then reassembled to form patterns, e.g. the letters of FORSYTHIA form a base for an acrostic lying on its side: FORSYTHIA OUT RACE SPRING'S YELLOW TELEGRAM HOPE INSISTS ACTION, which also makes the shape of a pot, and from this base the single letters, on thin stems made from their Morse-code signs, spring up in curves like those of a forsythia bush! Witty, ingenious, meaningful, and, I think, pretty if not beautiful—but no one could recite, memorize, or for that matter parse, such a creation.

Much concrete poetry is less 'comprehensible', extremely abstract; some practitioners incorporate bits of drawing or even photographs, or create abstract patterns with letters. These can give pleasure. John Furnival devised what at first looks like a grille, but on closer inspection is made up

[1] I use the word here in the sense of typographical *founts*, but the accidental pun is rather happy!

mostly of interlaced A's and Ω's: Alpha and Omega, the beginning and the end, are one, a recognized Christian image. Stephen Bann's *Amber Sands* is a page thickly sprinkled with ampersands printed in yellow. The interested reader should explore further, but not seeking the experiences usually expected of poetry.

Probably more widely important in our own century has been a breaking down of numerous taboos, accelerated since 1961 when the legal ban on *Lady Chatterley's Lover* was lifted. The change has not been merely towards a greatly improved recognition of realities and complexities about sex, but a move away from many kinds of hypocrisy, pretence and those sentimentalities that in operation can be very callous. In poetry there has been a parallel move away from what the critic A. L. Alvarez has called 'gentility'. The poet now has broader possibilities in subject-matter, in the treatment of the subjects, and in vocabulary.

I am prepared to stand up and be counted as at least Permissive enough to be thankful that the Prohibitive Society in which I was brought up has loosened its grip. Reading Jack Beckett's *The Keen Edge*, a collection of poems written by teenagers in school, apparently with no intent to shock or defy, I tried to imagine what would have happened in my schooldays if some of us had written with such candour about our real feelings and preoccupations. My imagination failed; I do not know how so huge, so harrowing, so resounding a row could have been contained in that school building.

The idea that no subject is in itself unsuitable for poetry has by now probably gained fairly general acceptance. Among numerous reasonably good poems that would have been impossible for general circulation forty years ago are

Auden's *The Geography of the House*, about the lavatory; George Macbeth's *A Confession*, about an abortion; Charles Causley's *Ballad of the Bread Man*, a moving but unusual religious poem which would have been heard as blasphemous; the fierce poems of Austin Clarke attacking opponents of contraception; Alasdair Maclean's *James Mackenzie*, about the pitiable but frightening lust of a village imbecile.

All kinds of subjects, including many traditional ones, can be treated with varieties of realism only recently acceptable. Could this, recognizable as, at least sometimes, true:

> David my son, my loved rival,
> And Julia, my tapering daughter,
> Now grant me one achievement only:
> I turn their wine to water.
>
> VERNON SCANNELL, *Silver Wedding*

have been admitted by a Victorian papa?

Falstaff is a funny fatty, and gluttons have been treated with scathing contempt; but Philip Hobsbaum's *Monologue of a Fat Man* brings out the tragic element in gross obesity. Philip Larkin's horrible but brilliant exploration of senility, *The Old Fools*, is a new way of handling the ancient theme of our mutability. The title of John Press's *January and May* evokes the traditional comic interpretations, especially Chaucer's, of old man with young bride; but Press, acknowledging the risks and ridiculous aspect, affirms the elements of marvellous rejuvenation and delight. In the long tradition of elegy, Edwin Brock writes *In Memory of my Father*, but begins, honestly and sadly:

> This is to please someone I never
> consciously pleased. . . .

and his *In Memory of my Grandmother* finds a tragic, complex symbolism in her last independent senile act, of lighting a fire in the wrong place.

The very frank treatment of personal experiences is nowadays sometimes placed in the special category of *confessional poetry*. Poems directly recounting personal feelings and experience are not, of course, new: we may think of some of Catullus, Shakespeare's sonnets, some of Donne, Byron, Elizabeth Barrett Browning, with *The Prelude* perhaps supreme. Modern confessional poetry often extends, however, to undisguised family problems, medical and psychiatric detail, or scraps of those exact concrete details that seem trivial but make things real:

> I wear bunny pink slippers in the hall.
>
> ANNE SEXTON, *The Operation*

Notable writers of confessional poetry include Anne Sexton, Robert Lowell, Elizabeth Jennings, Sylvia Plath, David Holbrook.

Vocabulary is now virtually unrestricted: medical and other scientific terminology, dialect words, colloquialisms, slang, even drastic swearing, appear in work by good poets. Any fool can try to startle by heaping up sexual swear-words instead of painfully selecting the thought-out epithet that is startlingly and exactly right; but even the brutal sexual insult is appropriate in Auden's *Song of the Devil* exactly where one might expect the Devil *would* use it, or Larkin's *This Be the Verse*; Auden and Larkin are so careful in their choice of words that their use of the outrageous is a real, purposeful choice. Martin Bell in his savage *Headmaster: Modern Style* uses vocabulary ranging from slang ('snitch', 'stung for expensive equipment') to unusual literary words ('mannikin', 'burgess', 'concupiscence')—and it works. George Macbeth in *Noah's Journey* makes the thunder talk not Sanskrit as in *The Waste Land*, but back-street:

> Talk big, small man, while you
> can. I will bash you.

—Again, it works, in its context. The poet's task is to choose the best word for the particular job, so a huge vocabulary, with a wide range of tones and implications, is ideal equipment.

Though I cannot quote statistical evidence to support a strong general impression, I think that in the last three decades there has been some lowering of the barriers between poets and poetry, and the non-specialist public.

There are several aspects of this. Eliot and Pound no longer dominate the scene with their poetry appealing mostly to a highly cultured and cerebral minority: poets as admirable and as diverse as, for example, Vernon Scannell, Philip Larkin, Kingsley Amis, Anne Ridler, D. J. Enright, Karen Gershon, Elizabeth Jennings. Ted Hughes, Tony Connor, can be genuinely enjoyed and for the most part understood by a much wider readership.

While the publishing of new poetry is notoriously unprofitable, with new volumes of poetry, or specialist poetry magazines, usually selling in miserable hundreds in our population of nearly sixty millions, the public now shows some appetite for poetry presented in media other than print. Public figures include poems in radio programmes such as 'With Great Pleasure'; short request programmes of poetry are broadcast. There are some poetry programmes on television, and the common television practice of using *one* well recited poem to close an evening's programme may be making people more aware of poetry as pleasure. Public readings by living poets in person, or by able reciters, have become more common, and have broken away from environments that some people find intimidatingly academic: we have poetry readings in pubs, poetry read to the accompaniment of jazz or as part of mixed programmes of poetry and jazz or other music; huge poetry festivals in the Albert Hall, provincial poetry competitions, Poetry Olympics at the Young Vic (which in 1981 were packed out). W. H. Smith, the chain of booksellers, has since 1971 sponsored 'Poets in School', through which over a hundred and fifty poets have visited schools to discuss poetry writing with pupils.

Today's senior citizens remember a time when the sophisticated musical entertainment of middle-class educated audiences included the wit, allusiveness and elegance of lyrics by Ira Gershwin, Cole Porter and, above all, Noel Coward; but mass audiences were often fed on insipid music and words of wretched fatuity. Since the end of the Second World War songs for mass consumption have developed interestingly: though drivel abounds for those who want it, the best of both the pop singers and the contemporary folk singers have often produced lyrics that may be recognized as poetry of a sort—not fatuous, not flavourless, and showing some real verbal skills and literary techniques. These intelligent songs appeal to a wide range of listeners, chiefly, though not exclusively, teenagers, and enable thousands who could not respond to poetry as presented in school to enjoy what is, in fact, an experience of poetry, though (as almost all sung poetry must be), a poetry of limited complexity and range of techniques. If we compare some *good* specimens with the words of many anthologized Elizabethan madrigals or lute songs, we may well find as much content, as interesting imagery and at least as worth-while comments on life in the modern songwriters. We may consider, for example, the best songs of the Beatles; still more, of Tom Paxton, Bob Dylan, Jake Thackray, Joni Mitchell, Harvey Andrews, David Buskin, Leon Rossel-son, or Ralph McTell with his forlorn old woman:

> 'She's got no time for talking,
> She just keeps right on walking,
> Carrying her home in two carrier-bags.'
>
> *The Streets of London*

Several songwriters, such as Leonard Cohen and Sydney Carter, have had volumes published as poetry, without music. Popular entertainer Spike Milligan writes appealing verses with some touch of poetic quality; we have, for rather smaller and more sophisticated audiences, such pleasures as the sung poems of Alasdair Clayre; the polished comic or satirical songs of Michael Flanders and Donald Swann; the sung satire of the 'Instant Sunshine' radio singers.

It is significant, too, that the *Radio Times* regularly pub-lishes the good verse pastiches—sometimes rather more than pastiches—of Roger Woddis, and that in the very popular television programme 'That's Life!' a favourite item was the satirical verse complaint (to the Inland Revenue, Gas Board, a peccant company, and so on) to which the offenders presented a witty reply in verse, with dance and music; not the 'immortal verse' Milton thought of, but keeping before us the idea of using verse as part of our everyday weaponry in the struggle for survival. Even limericks and rhyming graffiti demand some sort of craftsmanship.

The continuing, probably increasing, appeal of some of the most rudimentary, frivolous or ephemeral kinds of poetry, and of poetry readings, may have had some influence on many poets whose work is on a much higher artistic level; in our present epoch there seems to be an abundance of poetry that treats of serious topics with an apparently light touch—with irony, playfulness, colloquialism, flippancy, word-games, anecdotes; we can enjoy it at a first reading, even perhaps a first hearing, though further study will uncover some deeper implications, sometimes pathetic or even tragic. If, in avoiding pretentiousness or bombast, and trying to avoid emotional self-deceits, poets have to avoid some of the depths and heights and sublimity, we can have a great many other things that are worth having and meet human needs. That Kathleen Raine's *On a Deserted Shore* was the poetry that most helped me to find my way through the most rending bereavement I have experienced does not mean that I cannot enjoy John Fuller's *Cannibals and Missionaries*; they differ as much as chalk from cheese, but chalk and cheese are both very useful items.

Tastes quite legitimately differ, fluctuate, and also develop with experience. The total body of English poetry is a magnificent collection that offers rich nourishment for every stage of experience, level of perception, and personal taste. Any literate person can find some poetry to enjoy; later, the possibilities for more complex pleasures, increased by more careful study, are inexhaustible.

Let me end this book, not with an abstract generalization, but with one practical plea. It is very simple.

PLEASE BUY POEMS.

Poetry is one of the most skilled uses of language. Its pleasures are among the keenest that language can offer. It generally sells very badly; so today poetry is usually the worst-paid form of serious authorship. A poet is not an ethereal creature that feeds on honey-dew, but needs to eat and dress and pay electricity bills like the rest of us, and, very likely, has dependants; and, though authors cannot expect to have everything made easy for them, and anyone who has never worried about earning a living, or done uncongenial duties, does not know much about normal human experience, it is also true that the more of himself or herself an author has to give to other tasks and boring material worries, the less energy and will and time are left for the exacting art.

Publishers, too, have to eat. Good publishers sometimes risk losing on exceptionally good books not likely to sell well; but they cannot do it often. Booksellers have to run their businesses at a profit.

Thus vicious circles appear. Not many people buy books by living poets; so few bookshops find it worthwhile to keep a varied stock of good current poetry, and any they do have is unlikely to be well displayed; so people who might be tempted to buy do not see anything to tempt them, and, unless they are specialist students, have little idea what is available; so booksellers find there is no demand for poetry . . .

So, naturally, they tell publishers there is no demand for poetry; publishers print fewer volumes of poetry; popular cheap papers rarely review poetry; so the non-specialist public sees even less about poetry and is less likely to seek new work in the bookshops . . . The poets have a thin time and may also feel more inclined to write for a tiny, erudite readership. The art in which Britain has excelled suffers, and several million people miss pleasures they could in fact enjoy. Yet a good book is a good buy; we still have it when we have enjoyed it; we can read it many times; it is no trouble to maintain; it can even be sold, or make a decent present, if we are tired of it.

Many good publishers have had to stop publishing new poetry. Others will have to stop, if they cannot sell it. If we want British poetry to go on developing with fresh excitements—we, the reading public, have to help. Most of us could manage to buy at least one volume a year; some, one a month. Information (e.g. papers with reviews of poetry) can be found in public libraries; and those who truly cannot buy books can at least ask for them in the library; that is some help.

As a schoolgirl, I was a timid, anxious creature, bullied and afraid of stepping out of line. One day I was going to the hairdresser and taking a book to read under the drier. A friend asked me what it was; I showed him. 'For goodness's sake,' he warned me, 'don't take *poetry*! Anything but that! Don't let people *see* you reading poetry; they'll think you're *nuts*.'

Somehow, for once I did *not* shrivel into miserable conformity. I doubt whether the village hairdresser much improved the outside of my head, but under the drier I at least put something good inside my head—something to remain a joy now that my hair is grey.

It is unlikely that anyone reading this book is more crushed and cowardly than I was taught to be at school. All of us nowadays who will stand up and declare our love of poetry, and make some small sacrifices sometimes to buy it, are—by our support—helping to create it.

SUGGESTIONS FOR FURTHER READING

Those of us, most of all, who write books about literature, and, secondly, those who study for examinations about literature, should never forget that even the best literary criticism is nothing in comparison with a piece of great literature.

Literary criticism can help to improve our sensitivity. If I am gazing at a beautiful landscape, and a guide tells me 'those are poplars', or lends me binoculars, saying 'look down there, at the walled garden, and see the peacocks', or shows me on an ordnance map where we are, my enjoyment is, probably, increased; but the guide cannot create the landscape—or even the eyes.

Poetry is the most important reading-matter for anyone who wants to know about poetry.

A reading-list of English poetry worth reading would fill another book the size of this. The reader who wants to enlarge a beginner's interest in poetry may find anthologies helpful; we must eventually form our own taste, but we cannot do so without a lot of sampling.

Oxford University Press has for decades provided anthologies that are broad in scope, and scholarly, with printing and binding so beautiful that these add to our pleasure. There are twelve volumes that form a magnificent history of English poetry, written in examples:

The Oxford Book of English Verse, ed. Arthur Quiller-Couch, 1900, still in print, but largely superseded now by

The New Oxford Book of English Verse, 1250–1950, ed. Helen Gardner, 1972, a splendid volume from which to start.

The Oxford Book of Mediaeval Verse, ed. Celia and Kenneth Sisam, 1970. Some readers may be deterred from this excellent volume by language difficulties; but why not try? The most difficult words are glossed. Not, however, the best place to start.

The Oxford Book of Ballads, ed. Arthur Quiller-Couch, 1910.

The Oxford Book of Carols, ed. Percy Dearmer, R. Vaughan-Williams and Martin Shaw, 1928. (Includes all the tunes.)

The Oxford Book of Sixteenth-Century Verse, ed. E. K. Chambers, 1932.

The Oxford Book of Seventeenth-Century Verse, ed. H. J. C. Grierson and C. Bullough, 1934.

The Oxford Book of Eighteenth-Century Verse, ed. David Nichol Smith, 1926.

The Oxford Book of Nineteenth-Century English Verse,[1] ed. John Hayward, 1964.

The Oxford Book of Modern Verse 1892–1935, ed. W. B. Yeats, 1936.

The Oxford Book of Twentieth-Century English Verse, ed. Philip Larkin, 1973.

The Oxford Book of Contemporary Verse 1945–1980, ed. D. J.

[1] The student may find nineteenth-century poetry second-hand under the titles *The Oxford Book of Regency Verse*, later called *The Oxford Book of Romantic Verse*, and *The Oxford Book of Victorian Verse*—all genuine, but no longer being reprinted.

Enright, 1980. (Includes some English verse from Australia, Canada, India, Ireland, New Zealand, Trinidad, USA, as well as Britain.)

To this basic collection we may very usefully add:

The Oxford Book of Scottish Verse, ed. John MacQueen and Tom Scott, 1966.
The Oxford Book of American Verse, ed. F. O. Mathiessen, 1957.
The Oxford Book of Children's Verse, ed. Iona and Peter Opie, 1973. (Great fun for grown-ups, too!)
The Oxford Book of Satirical Verse, ed. Geoffrey Grigson, 1980.
The Oxford Book of Light Verse, ed. W. H. Auden, 1938.
The New Oxford Book of Light Verse, ed. Kingsley Amis, 1978. Auden and Amis differed enormously in their approaches, and both achieved splendid collections which complement each other.
The Oxford Book of Verse in English Translation, ed. Charles Tomlinson, 1981.

The other publishing company that has of recent years made poetry much more accessible to the public is Penguin Books at Harmondsworth, who in a relatively short time have brought out seriously edited and pleasantly produced volumes of many poets of the past—among them Blake, Browning, Donne, Hardy, Jonson, Kipling, Marvell, Vaughan and Wyatt; many volumes of twentieth-century poetry; a considerable collection of the poetry of other nations; and numerous anthologies, which include:

The Penguin Book of English Verse, ed. John Hayward, 1956.

The Penguin Book of American Verse, ed. Geoffrey Moore, 1977.
Comic and Curious Verse, ed. J. M. Cohen, 1952.
The Penguin Book of Ballads, ed. Geoffrey Grigson, 1975.
The Common Muse (English ballad poetry), ed. V. de Sola Pinto and A. E. Rodway, 1965 (pub. by Chatto & Windus, 1957).
Love Poetry, ed. Jon Stallworthy, 1976 (pub. by Allen Lane, 1973).
The Penguin Book of Women Poets, ed. Carol Cosman, Joan Keefe and Kathleen Weaver, 1980. Includes many beautiful translations (pub. by Allen Lane, 1978).
The Penguin Book of Elizabethan Verse, ed. Edward Lucie-Smith, 1965.
The Metaphysical Poets, ed. Helen Gardner, 1957.
The Penguin Book of Restoration Verse, ed. Harold Love, 1968.
The Penguin Book of Eighteenth-Century Verse, ed. Dennis Davison, 1973.
The Penguin Book of English Romantic Verse, ed. David Wright, 1968.
The Penguin Book of Victorian Verse, ed. George Macbeth, 1969.
Georgian Poetry, ed. James Reeves, 1962.
The Penguin Book of First World War Poetry, ed. Jon Silkin, 1979.
Imagist Poetry, ed. Peter Jones, 1972.
Longer Contemporary Poems, ed. David Wright, 1966.
Poetry of the Thirties, ed. Robin Skelton, 1964.
Contemporary Verse, ed. Kenneth Allott, 1950.
Contemporary American Poetry, ed. Donald Hall, 1962.
The New Poetry, ed. A. Alvarez, 1962.

British Poetry since 1945, ed. Edward Lucie-Smith, 1970.

There are dozens of other anthologies: selections from periods of literature, of types of literature, on specific topics; anthologies for specialist students, for schools, for the coffee-table. Some good ones include:

Everyman's Book of English Verse, ed. John Wain, Dent, London, 1981. As far as I know, this is now the most inclusive and instructive one-volume anthology; it extends from translations from Old English to Seamus Heaney, Brian Patten and Peter Levi, and is better on the mediaeval period than most general anthologies; it also includes a long and interesting introductory essay.

My second choice for one large single-volume anthology would be:

Poetry of the English-Speaking World, ed. Richard Aldington, Heinemann, 1947. A good broad selection in chronological order.

The Golden Treasury of English Lyric Poetry, ed. Francis Turner Palgrave, 1861, second series 1896. Probably the most famous of all anthologies of English poetry. It has been reprinted, often with additions, many times, e.g. Everyman series, Dent, 1906; Everyman Paperback, 1955, and Oxford University Press, 1964, with a substantial 'fifth book' by John Press. 'Palgrave' must in his day have made an incalculable contribution to the love of poetry in Britain; but his taste was so narrow (no Donne, Blake, or any of his own contemporaries) that he at the same time was responsible for narrowing public taste considerably.

A Little Treasury of Modern Poetry, ed. Oscar Williams, Routledge & Kegan Paul, London, 1947. ('Little' in format rather than in content.) Broad, interesting, and sometimes unexpected.

Poetry of the Present, ed. Geoffrey Grigson, Phoenix House, London, 1949. Useful in representing some good minor poets not very well known.

Cambridge Book of English Verse 1900–39, ed. Allen Freer and John Andrew, Cambridge University Press, 1970. Substantial selections from the eleven poets the editors regarded as most significant, with very full notes and some biographical and bibliographical information.

Cambridge Book of English Verse 1939–1975, ed. Alan Bold, Cambridge University Press, 1976. Exactly similar structure to the previous volume; ten more poets, who in some cases themselves helped with the annotations.

Anthology of Modern Poetry, ed. John Wain, Hutchinson, London, 1963. A good assorted non-sectarian collection, with some useful notes.

Anthology of Contemporary Poetry: Post-War to the Present, ed. John Wain, Hutchinson, London, 1979. A very good collection, broad in scope and with plenty of non-obvious items; sensible notes on the poets, and some useful annotations. Might well prod the torpid reader awake again.

SHOCK THERAPY

The reader whose appetite for poetry has somehow failed, or who has never had an appetite, may possibly be jolted out of apathy by one of these unusual anthologies:

The Penguin Book of Sick Verse, ed. George Macbeth, Penguin, 1963. Poetry of 'the extreme situation'; rather a lot of nineteenth-century decadence, and some quite difficult poems, but a good unusual mix for dipping.

A Personal Choice, ed. John Wain, David & Charles, Newton Abbot, London, 1978. Some unexpected items and a very stimulating introduction.

The Penguin Book of Unrespectable Verse, ed. Geoffrey Grigson, 1980 (first pub. Allen Lane, 1971). A very assorted assortment indeed, not just cheeky, but often really thought-provoking.

Billy the Kid: An Anthology of Tough Verse, ed. Michael Baldwin, Hutchinson, London, 1963. A wide range of poems of strong excitement or bitter humour; might stimulate someone who has been dosed with poetry felt as wishy-washy or 'good for you'.

Strictly Private, ed. Roger McGough, Kestrel Books, Penguin, Harmondsworth, 1981. An unexpected choice of fresh, mildly shocking, often disturbingly true, contemporary verse. An editor who can include in his foreword, 'and anyway, what are you doing messing about in my preface when you should be over the page and in amongst the real stuff?' is at least not dispensing boredom pills.

Making Love, ed. Alan Bold, The Picador Book of Erotic Verse, Picador Pan Books, London, 1978. A very mixed collection; includes some erotic verse so explicitly physiological that it could upset some readers; but may remind others that not all the poetry of sexual love is wistful yearning, and that polished craftsmanship can shine on any topic.

The Bawdy Beautiful, ed. Alan Bold, The Sphere Book of Improper Verse, Sphere Books, 1979. A startling anthology with a sensible introduction; some duplication from the previous anthology; some coarser matter from surreptitious oral tradition. Could genuinely distress some readers, or do harm to some kinds of immature mind; but might be a drastic antidote for someone suffering from a premature overdose of golden daffodils and corners of a foreign field.

REFERENCE BOOKS

The Princeton Encyclopaedia of Poetry and Poetics, ed. Alex Preminger, Princeton University Press, 1965; enlarged ed. 1974. As far as I know, this is the fullest reference book in English devoted wholly to poetry. Its scope is worldwide; it should shake anyone's insularity. Deals not with particular authors or poems, but the history, theory, technique and criticism of poetry, from the earliest recorded beginnings. Many very valuable articles, e.g. on 'Imagery', 'Metaphor', 'Symbol'; but assumes that the reader already has a wide literary culture. Includes many rare verse forms and figures of speech.

Cassell's Encyclopaedia of World Literature, ed. S. H. Steinberg, Cassell, London, 2 vols, 1953; Revised ed. J. Buchanan-Brown, 3 vols, 1973. An ample, valuable reference book, useful not least as a humbling reminder of how vast is the subject and how little one person can know. Many general articles useful to the student of poetry, e.g. 'Ballad', 'Metaphysical Poetry', 'Ode', 'Prosody'.

Babette Deutsch, *Poetry Handbook; A Dictionary of Terms*, Funk & Wagnalls, New York, 1957, or Cape, London, 1958. Terms relevant to verse in the English language; very clear, with useful examples. Particularly thorough on the classification of rhymes.

J. A. Cuddon, *A Dictionary of Literary Terms*, Andre Deutsch, 1977, is the fullest of such dictionaries, with many items not often glossed.

K. Beckson and A. Ganz, *A Reader's Guide to Literary Terms*, Thames & Hudson, 1961, is a good second choice.

Roger Fowler, *A Dictionary of Modern Critical Terms*, Routledge & Kegan Paul, London, 1973, is helpful on modern developments in criticism.

A FEW ENGLISH CLASSICS ABOUT POETRY

selected for permanent value and historical interest.

George Puttenham, *The Arte of English Poesie*, 1589, edited by Gladys Doidge Willcock and Alice Walker, Cambridge University Press, 1936.

Sir Philip Sidney, *A Defence of Poetrie* (sometimes known as *An Apologie for Poetrie*), 1595, edited by Katherine Duncan-Jones and Jan van Dorsten, in *Miscellaneous Prose of Sir Philip Sidney*, Oxford University Press, 1973. (A large part of Puttenham's book, Sidney's *Defence*, and many other interesting early works may be found in

Elizabethan Critical Essays, ed. G. Gregory Smith, 2 vols, Oxford University Press, 1904.)

Alexander Pope, *Essay on Criticism*, 1711. To be found in any edition of Pope's poems, e.g. *Poetical Works*, ed. Herbert Davies, Oxford University Press, 1966.

Samuel Johnson, *Lives of the Poets*, 1779–81. Available in several modern editions, e.g. World's Classics, 2 vols, Oxford University Press, 1906.

William Wordsworth, Preface to *Lyrical Ballads*, 1798. Accessible in several editions of *Lyrical Ballads*, e.g. that by R. L. Brett and A. R. Jones, Methuen, London, 1963.

William Wordsworth, *The Prelude*, 'The Growth of a Poet's Mind', preferably in the 1805 version, ed. E. de Selincourt, Oxford University Press, 1933.

S. T. Coleridge, *Biographia Literaria*, 1817. Several modern editions, e.g. the Everyman edition, ed. George Watson, Dent, London, or Dutton, New York, revised eds 1965, 1975.

P. B. Shelley, *A Defence of Poetry*, 1821. In the *Prose Works*, ed. R. H. Shepherd, Chatto & Windus, London, 1888, or in *Peacock's 'Four Ages of Poetry', Shelley's 'Defence of Poetry' and Browning's 'Essay on Shelley'*, ed. H. F. Brett-Smith, Blackwells, Oxford, 1921.

PROSODY AND VERSE FORMS

Robert Bridges, *Milton's Prosody*, Oxford University Press, Oxford, 1921. Not a beginner's book; and should not be gulped and swallowed whole; may perplex the reader not brought up on the classics, who is never tempted to think about quantity; but for the careful reader, throws a flood of light on English prosody in general, e.g. on the numerous variations on the basic iambic pentameter.

G. S. Fraser, *Metre, Rhyme and Free Verse*, Methuen, London, 1970. A very clear, helpful handbook, particularly praiseworthy in its treatment of the frequent ambiguities in metre. Recommended for both beginners and those who wish to advance further. Friendly, small and not noisily dogmatic.

Harvey Gross, *Sound and Form in Modern Poetry: A study of prosody from Thomas Hardy to Robert Lowell*, University of Michigan Press, Ann Arbor, 1964. Thorough, full of valuable information, much of which is not easy to find elsewhere; strongly recommended to the lover of poetry who wants a better understanding of recent developments; but not for the novice.

Ernst Haüblein, *The Stanza* (Critical Idiom series), Methuen, London, 1978. Very thorough; recommended to those who enjoy factual technical detail so full as almost to suggest mathematics; well shows the complexity of the poet's craft; too much for the novice.

Gerard Manley Hopkins, *Poems*, ed. Robert Bridges, Oxford University Press, enlarged second edn, 1930. The short 'Author's Preface' is a key document on experimental prosody, and should be studied, of course, in conjunction with the poems.

Catherine Ing, *Elizabethan Lyrics*, Chatto & Windus, London, 1951. Of interest to students not of the Elizabethan period only; includes a very valuable chapter on prosodic terms, but unique in its deep and subtle examination of the relationship between poetry and music. Not easy reading, especially for the non-musical, but very revealing.

James MacAuley, *A Primer of English Versification*, Sydney, 1966. Short, clear and sensible.

George Saintsbury, *Historical Manual of English Prosody*, Macmillan, London, 1910. Does not go beyond Swinburne, and its style now seems heavily old-fashioned, but still an important book for anyone wanting to go into the subject in any depth.

Karl Shapiro and Robert Beum, *A Prosody Handbook*, Harper & Row, New York and London, 1965. Very thorough; includes a chapter on classical prosody and a useful glossary; lucidly and urbanely written.

THE LANGUAGE OF POETRY

Owen Barfield, *Poetic Diction*, Faber & Gwyer, London, 1928; Wesleyan University Press, Middletown, Connecticut, 1973. Barfield's bent was philosophical, but the reader whose interests lie elsewhere can still learn something from his exploration of the poet's use of language.

R. P. Blackmur, *Language as Gesture*, Allen & Unwin, London, 1954. Emphatically not for the novice; worth an effort for the experienced student of poetry.

Christine Brooke-Rose, *A Grammar of Metaphor*, Secker & Warburg, London, 1965. A minute examination of nuances of poetic metaphor, classified by grammatical definitions. Not a novice read, but may help the serious student to look harder at poetic language and how it works.

C. Day Lewis, *The Poetic Image*, Cape, London, 1947. A well-written, well-illustrated study of imagery, with some interesting matter also about the creative process.

Helpful to the comparative beginner, but unlikely to be outgrown.

Terence Hawkes, *Metaphor* (Critical Idiom series), Methuen, London, 1972. Interesting, clearly written survey of changing ideas about metaphor; useful reading-list.

Winifred Nowottny, *The Language Poets Use*, University of London, Athlone Press, London, and University of Toronto Press, Oxford University Press in New York, 1962. One of the best books for the serious student on the language of poetry; notable for excellent examples and handling of the examples. Makes fairly severe demands on the reader, but gives a lot in return.

HELP WITH TWENTIETH-CENTURY POETRY

Thomas Blackburn, *The Price of an Eye*, Longmans, London, 1961. A sensible, serious and well-written book on a large number of modern poets, up to the 1950s.

Babette Deutsch, *Poetry in our Time*, New York, 1956 (first pub. 1952). A substantial, zestful and often very helpful broad survey of poetry 1900–56, in Britain, Ireland and USA, with a great many stimulating examples. The style is for the moment unfashionable, but fashions pass; a book to broaden experience of poetry.

George Fraser, *Vision and Rhetoric: Studies in Modern Poetry*, Faber & Faber, London, 1959. Studies of eleven twentieth-century poets; many interesting perceptions that can help others to be more perceptive.

Martin Gilkes, *A Key to Modern English Poetry*, Blackie, London and Glasgow, 1937, second edn, 1945. Easy reading for the beginner, but needs to be read cautiously, since it is now very much out-of-date, notably on Auden, Spender and Day Lewis.

J. Isaacs, *The Background of Modern Poetry*, Bell, London, 1951. A useful little book, written when Eliot was the dominant figure.

John Livingston Lowes, *Convention and Revolt in Poetry*, Constable, London, 1919. This sane, pleasant, readable little book is still not out of date; the reader should remember that it was written in the epoch of the Imagists, but it contains much permanent good sense about tradition and innovation, fashion, topicality and aspects of poetic diction.

Margaret O'Donnell, *Feet on the Ground, being an Approach to Modern Verse*, Blackie, London and Glasgow, 1946. A very elementary, but very sensible, guide for the novice, with plenty of examples. But note the date. Suggests a wise humility in approaching the unfamiliar, and some sensible ideas about discriminating.

John Press, *Rule and Energy: Trends in British Poetry since the Second World War*, Oxford University Press, 1963. A very good general sketch of the epoch, trying to be fair, and fairly catholic; good examples and a very good reading list.

Margaret Schlauch, *Modern English and American Poetry: Techniques and Ideologies*, Watts, London, 1956. This study, written, apparently, at Warsaw University, by a moderate Marxist, may need to be read with the salt-cellar to hand for taking a pinch with some of the views on the poet and society; but it also contains some intelligent general observations, and really intelligent material about various language techniques, with a close study of sound effects.

James Scully (ed.), *Modern Poetics*, McGraw-Hill, New York, Toronto, San Francisco, 1965. Essays on poetry by fourteen important modern poets, and one interview. Very interesting; its value is perhaps above all that it shows how very different, as well as sometimes how very similar, can be the attitudes and methods of various poets who have won deserved fame.

Yvor Winters, *In Defense of Reason*, Routledge & Kegan Paul, London, 1960 (New York, 1937). Only the first 150 pages treat of poetry. A very polemical, rather unsympathetic book, recommended only to experienced, confident enjoyers of poetry; but it is written out of wide knowledge, and does ask some real questions, and make some real points, some of them unfashionable, that at least deserve consideration; and it offers arguments and evidence, not just tutting and snarling.

SELECTED GENERAL CRITICAL WORKS

(The reader who wants more can find much more; this is a short list of some of the books most likely to improve understanding of poetry without infecting the reader with much critical jargon.)

W. H. Auden, *The Dyer's Hand*, Faber & Faber, London, 1963, paperback, 1975. Thought-provoking, splendidly individual. Worth finding, above all, for Auden's 'daydream College for Bards', with its many stimulating implications.

John Bayley, *The Romantic Survival: A Study in Poetic Evolution*, Constable, London, 1957. Extremely interesting; not for the novice. A critical work that includes the reminder: 'All slogans, explanations and critical catchphrases by poets and their critics suffer from being almost impossible to relate to the actuality of poetry itself.' (p.60) is likely to be a wise book!

Maud Bodkin, *Archetypal Patterns in Poetry: Psychological Studies of Imagination*, Oxford University Press, 1934, reprinted 1963, 1965. Interesting to those interested in the deeper content of great poetry—psychological, philosophical, religious; written from a psychoanalytical viewpoint, but without pretentious jargon or clique dogmatism.

C. M. Bowra, *The Background of Modern Poetry*, Oxford University Press, 1946. Though this single lecture is now somewhat dated, it remains a miniature masterpiece as a lesson on how to approach some new, unfamiliar kind of poetry.

Christopher Caudwell, *Illusion and Reality*, Macmillan, London, 1937. Marxist criticism can be hideously narrow and jargon-clotted; this classic of Marxist criticism is exceptionally well-written and offers many interesting ideas. Not for the novice.

C. Day Lewis, *Poetry for You*, Blackwell, Oxford, 1944. Written in very simple language to help children to enjoy poetry; but a good start for the real beginner adult.

T. S. Eliot, *Selected Prose of T. S. Eliot*, ed. Frank Kermode, Faber & Faber, London, 1975. At least the general essays, 'Tradition and the Individual Talent', 'The Function of Criticism', 'The Music of Poetry' and 'What is a Classic?' should be read; they are of permanent interest as products of a fine, fastidious mind.

William Empson, *Seven Types of Ambiguity*, Chatto & Windus, London, 1930, revised edn, 1947. *The Structure of Complex Words*, Chatto & Windus, London, 1951. Not for novices, but enormously exciting for the reader who is ready for them. Empson's criticism is difficult, unusual, and so interesting that one can be tempted to swallow it whole and incur a one-sided bulge; but it is genuinely enlightening to any serious student of poetry.

Robert Graves, *On English Poetry*, Heinemann, London, 1922; *The Common Asphodel*, Hamish Hamilton, London, 1949 (includes some abridged material from *On English Poetry*). The reader should approach Graves's critical works—especially some not mentioned here—with some caution; they are often explosive. Many of his views are very controversial; but it is not necessary to adopt all of his opinions to find a great deal of interest and stimulus in his essays; and they are blessedly lucid.

T. R. Henn, *The Apple and the Spectroscope*, Methuen, London, 1951. Lectures on poetry, intended to help those whose bent is originally scientific. Some very clear help with interpretation and much sensible general guidance.

John Livingston Lowes, *The Road to Xanadu*, Constable, London, 1927. A marvellously exciting exploration of how a poet (Coleridge) used raw material from his reading in his creative processes.

Peter V. Marinelli, *Pastoral* (Critical Idiom series), Methuen, London, 1971. A valuable study, not for beginners, of a genre more varied and complex than we always realize.

Edwin Muir, *The Estate of Poetry*, Hogarth Press, London, 1962. Six lectures that make some wise points on the function of criticism, the approach to poetry.

Ezra Pound, *Literary Essays*, ed. T. S. Eliot, Faber & Faber, London, 1954. Pound dogmatized colourfully and made no attempt to be fair to anyone not on his waveband, which was somewhat narrow. Eliot compares him to 'a man trying to convey to a very deaf person the fact that the house is on fire.' As a guru or tin god, Pound has sometimes been a destructive influence; but he really cared about poetry and was one of the best of critics for provoking readers to think.

John Press, *The Chequer'd Shade: Reflections on Obscurity in Poetry*, Oxford University Press, 1958, paperback, 1963. An excellent, sane, readable book on a difficult, controversial subject; recommended alike to perplexed novice and experienced reader.

Kathleen Raine, *Defending Ancient Springs*, Oxford University Press, 1967. An eloquent, passionate, but scholarly, exposition of how the great central mysteries of life, the spiritual dimension, are the material of truly great poetry. Though we may here and there suspect some overstating or too narrow defining, the book is eminently worth reading and a valuable antidote to more prevalent, more sterile dogmatisms.

I. A. Richards, *Practical Criticism*, Routledge & Kegan Paul, London, 1929. A detailed account of what happened when thirteen poems, without authors' names, were submitted to Cambridge students and comments invited. The extent to which highly literate, articulate readers could misunderstand, drag in irrelevant criteria or be pathetically trivial, is disquieting; but Richards offers many suggestions for improving our response.

I. A. Richards, *Principles of Literary Criticism*, Routledge & Kegan Paul, London, 1924. The beginner will find this intimidating, but it is very valuable to anyone ready for it.

Robin Skelton, *Poetry*, Teach Yourself Series, English

Universities Press, London, 1963. A fairly elementary handbook; but some quite deep understanding is communicated in lucid exposition. Particularly helpful on imagery and the poet's attitude to linguistic usage. The touch of humour here and there helps.

Robin Skelton, *The Practice of Poetry*, Heinemann, London, 1971. This is more a book on how to *write* poetry—an apprentice's handbook—than on reading it, but it tells any reader a lot about poetry. It is clear and human, without being shallow.

Robin Skelton, *The Poetic Pattern*, Routledge & Kegan Paul, London, 1956. A more difficult book; but difficult ideas are conveyed without pretentiousness or muddle. On the theme of poetry as 'patterned life'; interesting on the relationships of poetry to magic and science, the creative process, and imagery.

E. M. W. Tillyard, *Poetry Direct and Oblique*, Chatto & Windus, London, 1934, revised 1945. A very useful, readable, sensible little book that shows many beginners how to read poetry with deeper enjoyment.

Charles Williams, *The English Poetic Mind*, Oxford University Press, 1932. Mostly about Shakespeare, Milton and Wordsworth, but relevant to the general study of poetry; and interesting ideas are put over in very good prose.

FOR THE TEACHER

Michael Baldwin, *Poetry without Tears*, Routledge & Kegan Paul, London, 1959. Spirited, provocative book on poetry in schools, by an experienced teacher.

Jack Beckett, *The Keen Edge; An analysis of poems by adolescents*, Blackie, London and Glasgow, 1965. Includes a copious selection of actual poems by adolescents, often moving as human documents, though we must remember that all such poetry is by authors who are not yet even real apprentices to the craft.

Thomas Blackburn (ed.), *Presenting Poetry: A handbook for English teachers*, University of London Institute of Education, Methuen, London, 1956. Essays by fifteen experts, including practising poets as well as teachers. Much valuable, stimulating thought, also good practical details about books and records available, and an excellent reading list.

Victoria V. Brown (ed.), *The Experience of Poetry in School*, Oxford University Press, 1953. Six essays, by practising teachers, on presenting poetry in schools; useful realistic ideas.

John F. Danby, *Approach to Poetry*, Heinemann, London and Toronto, 1940. A sensible, realistic book, sound on the importance of enjoyment, and not without humour. Includes some clever ideas for putting concepts over in the classroom, and other practical teaching methods.

Robert Druce, *The Eye of Innocence: Children and their Poetry*, Brockhampton Press, Leicester, 1965. Mostly about encouraging children to write their own poetry; some very interesting material. I cannot resist quoting the child who discovered that a dog's nostrils look like inverted commas.

Marjorie L. Hourd, *The Education of the Poetic Spirit*, Heinemann, Melbourne, London, Toronto, 1949. Very interesting and stimulating, with fascinating examples drawn from classroom experience, discussed with some reference to psycho-analysis. The experience was, however, with girls who were at least literate, in a framework of civilized discipline, a situation many teachers may envy.

James Reeves, *Teaching Poetry*, Heinemann, London, 1958. By a practising teacher and poet. Short, sensible, realistic.

T. W. Sussams, *Poetry and the Teacher*, Nelson, London, Edinburgh, 1949. A useful book by an experienced teacher; painfully and helpfully realistic about difficulties and disappointments.

SOME SUGGESTIONS FOR LISTENING

We can often trace a dislike of poetry to hearing it read aloud badly by teachers, worse by classmates; or recited destructively by the uninterested or untalented or conceited.

Conversely, the uninterested may develop an interest, and almost any reader may grow in appreciation and understanding, by listening attentively to poetry spoken by adequate speakers.

Radio and television programmes of poetry are not numerous, but are worth seeking, and, when done, are often very well done.

There is today a considerable body of recorded poetry on discs or cassettes. Since there is not a mass demand, only really good record shops are likely to carry a reasonable stock of recorded poetry; but manufacturers will usually send a current list for a stamp to cover postage.

Companies that record poetry include the following:

Caedmon Spoken Word Records,
Teakfield,
1 Westmead,
Farnborough,
Hampshire GU14 7RU.

The claim of Caedmon to be 'building up a unique collection in sound of the greatest works of literature' is not unreasonable. The readers are normally either experienced actors and actresses, or the poets themselves. Poets in the Caedmon list interpreting their own works include: W. H. Auden, Sir John Betjeman, E. E. Cummings, Walter de la Mare, T. S. Eliot, Robert Frost, Robert Graves, Geoffrey Hill, Ted Hughes, Randall Jarrell, Robert Lowell, Archibald MacLeish, John Masefield, Marianne Moore, Brian Patten, Sylvia Plath, Ezra Pound, Anne Sexton, Edith Sitwell, Stephen Spender, Wallace Stevens and Dylan Thomas.

The Caedmon list includes not only a wide range of earlier poetry read by professionals, but records designed to help the teaching of poetry, and such extras as a recording of all the songs from Shakespeare's plays.

Argo Records,
A Division of the Decca Record Co., Ltd,
115 Fulham Road,
London SW3 6RR

have recorded the complete works of Shakespeare, with many outstanding players, and have a good collection of poetry.

Charisma Records, Ltd,
90 Wardour Street,
London W1V 3LE

have a few poetry records, chiefly by Sir John Betjeman.

Anvil Music,
36 Crescent Road,
Royal Tunbridge Wells,
Kent TN1 2LZ

sells story cassettes, mainly for children; these include light verse by Belloc, Carroll, Edward Lear and E. V. Rieu.

Saydisc Records,
The Barton,
Inglestone Common,
Badminton, Glos. GL9 1BX

have a few verse recordings of specialized interest.

Here is the place for a reminder that listening to poetry set to music can be a richly rewarding experience, and that a good deal of material is available on records, from the majestic, tragic *War Requiem* of Benjamin Britten, with ten poems by Wilfred Owen interwoven with a requiem mass, to Andrew Lloyd Webber's varied hilarious settings of the lighter Eliot for the musical show *Cats*. Besides beautiful works never envisaged by the poets, such as Vaughan Williams's settings of Blake and Housman or Britten's *Serenade for Tenor, Horn and Strings*, there are poems that were destined from the first for musical settings: Elizabethan madrigals and lute songs; carols, ballads and other folk-songs; songs from plays; hymns; light verse such as the libretti of W. S. Gilbert, the Flanders and Swann songs; the songs of various communities and groups. Many of the extracts from the Bible or liturgy that have been set to music for religious purposes, as for instance in oratorio, are also passages of sublime poetry.

INDEX

Absalom and Achitophel, 105
accentual verse, 195–8, 203
Acis and Galatea, 40
Address to a Haggis, 158
Adieu, farewell Earth's bliss . . ., 138
Adonais, 85, 106
Aeneid, 102
Age of Bronze, The, 48, 105
Airs and Madrigals, 49
Aldington, Richard, 162
Alexander Pope (E. Sitwell), 62
Alexandrine, 152
All women born . . ., 155
allegory, 143
Allegro, L', 8, 70, 170
alliteration, 5,65–73, 79, 179, 196, 204
Alternative Service Book, 90–1
Alvarez, A. L., 208
Amber Sands, 208
Amis, Kingsley, 59, 129, 156, 211
amphibrach, 25, 27
amphimacer, 25
anapaest, 24, 26, 42, 43, 201, 203
Anathemata, The, 164
Ancient Mariner, The, 47, 103, 150
Andrea del Sarto, 200
Andrews, Harvey, 213
Anglo-saxon, 66
Annus Mirabilis, 106
anthologies, 3, 107 (*and see* Suggestions for further reading)
Antony and Cleopatra, 173
Apes and Parrots, 96n.
apocopated rhyme, 55
Arcadia, 109
archy and mehitabel, 165
Arnold, Matthew, 103, 106, 109, 161
Arte of English Poesie, The, 12
Art of Healing, The, 202
As You Like It, 108
Ash Wednesday, 162

Ashcroft, Peggy, 4
associations, 7, 101, 124–36
assonance, 54, 65
At a Hasty Wedding, 155
At Parting, 13
At the Grave of Henry James, 202
Auden, Wystan Hugh, 54, 87n., 97–8, 103, 105, 106, 129, 140, 148, 149, 152, 155, 156, 158, 169, 187, 192, 197, 202, 203, 204, 209, 210
Autumn Journal, 104

Babylon, 93
Bacchus, 101
Back to the Army Again, 97
ballad, 46, 47n., 56, 92–3, 103–4, 143, 150, 204
Ballad of the Bread Man, 209
Ballad of the Long-legged Bait, 103
Ballad of Reading Gaol, 103
ballade, 153, 167
Ballade of the Cats of Bygone Time, 153
Ballade of the First Rain, A, 153
Ballade of the Hanged, 153
Ballade of Suicide, 153
Ballade to Queen Elizabeth, 153
Bann, Stephen, 208
Barker, George, 106, 187, 200
Barrack-room Ballads, 150
Bar-room Matins, 129
Battle of Maldon, The, 66
Battle of the Stories, The, 97
Beatles, 213
Beaumont, Francis, 109
Beckett, Jack, 208
Bedtime Story, 104
Bees' Nest, 166
Bell, C. D., 154
Bell, Martin, 210
Belloc, Hilaire, 158
Beowulf, 66
Beppo, 152
Beside the Seaside, 148
Betjeman, Sir John, 4, 105, 148, 187
Binnorie, 93
Bishop Orders his Tomb, The, 110
Blake, William, 2, 42, 59, 68, 102, 107, 114, 140, 141, 162, 192
blank verse, 49, 109, 148, 160
Blunden, Edmund, 53, 108
Boats and Places, 166
Bold, Alan, 166
Bone, Gavin, 66
Bothie of Tober-na-Vuolich, The, 157
Break, break, break . . ., 41
Breton, Nicholas, 157
Breve, 18, 22
Bridge of Sighs, The, 50
Bridges, Robert, 22, 23, 155, 157
Briggflatts, 164
Britten, Benjamin, 95
Brock, Edwin, 209
broken rhyme, 55
Brook, The, 59–60
Brooke, Rupert, 192
Brophy, John, 95n.
Brothers, The, 110

Browning, Elizabeth Barrett, 81, 151, 210
Browning, Robert, 48, 56, 110, 120, 132, 157, 158, 160, 173, 210
Bunting, Basil, 163, 164
Burghers, The, 150
Burns, Robert, 57, 76, 133, 137, 158
Buskin, David, 213
Butler, Samuel, 50, 149
Byron, Lord, 47, 48, 51, 52, 56, 80, 82, 85, 102, 105, 109, 136, 149, 150, 160, 186, 192, 210

caesura, 196
Caliban upon Setebos, 110
Call it a Good Marriage, 88
Calverley, C. S., 51
Campbell, Roy, 102, 140, 149
Campion, Thomas, 22, 49, 99, 161
Cannibals and Missionaries, 214
Canterbury Tales, The, 47
Cantos, The, 101, 164
Captain Scuttle Ashore, 110
carol, 7, 143, 144
Carter, Sydney, 213
Case, The, 162
Case of Murder, A, 104
Castle, The, 123
catalectic line, 30, 46
Catullus, 131, 210
Causley, Charles, 209
Chaffinch Map of Scotland, 204
chant royal, 153
Chaucer, Geoffrey, 47, 102, 114, 149, 152, 153, 154, 158, 209
Chesterton, G. K., 97, 153
Chickahanka, 94
Child is father to the man, The, 155
Childe Harold's Pilgrimage, 82, 152
choral speaking, 62, 94
Christmas Sermon, 57
Christopher Columbus, 109
Christ's Victory and Triumph, 102
Chronicle, The, 75–6
Church-Porch, The, 104
cinema, 164
cinquain, 158
Clare, John, 52, 82
Clarke, Austin, 209
classical education, 21, 86, 114
classical metres (*see also* hexameters, quantity), 21, 25, 29–30, 38, 40, 157, 161
Clayre, Alasdair, 213
Clerk's Tale, The, 103, 152
Clough, Arthur Hugh, 22, 157
Cohen, Leonard, 213
Coleridge, Hartley, 119
Coleridge, Samuel Taylor, 47, 69, 103, 150, 160
Colin Clout, 158, 160
Collins, William, 170
Colson, Greta, 22n.
Comfort, Alex, 106
Coming of Arthur, The, 61
common measure, 150
Computer's First Christmas Card, The, 166

Concrete Poetry, 13, 204–8
Confession, A, 209
Confessional Poetry, 210
Congo, The, 62
Connor, J. D., 22n.
Connor, Tony, 103, 166, 211
Consonances, 53
Constable, Henry, 84
counterpoint, 34, 181
Country Dance, 62
couplets, 47, 109, 149, 177
Coward, Noel, 212
Cowley, Abraham, 75–6
Cowper, William, 103, 148
Crabbe, George, 149
Crane, Walter, 153
Crashaw, Richard, 138
cretic, 25
critical vocabulary, 5–6, 110–11, 185
Cromwell, Oliver, 15
Cruel Mother, The, 92
Cummings, E. E., 165, 166, 205
curtal sonnet, 151
Cymbeline, 173

dactyl, 22, 23–4, 26, 29, 157, 201, 203
Daddyo, 165
Daniel, Samuel, 110, 151
Dante, 102, 150
Dare to be a Daniel, 4
Dark Tower, The, 109
Dauber, 103
Davenant, Sir William, 151
Davies, W. H., 25
Death and Doctor Hornbook, 158
Dedication, 150
Dekker, Thomas, 82
Deposed General, A, 166
Deserted Village, The, 108
Dialogue, A, 110, 154–5
Diamond Body, 162
Dickinson, Emily, 83
didactic poetry, 104–5, 112, 149, 181
dimeter, 26, 43, 181
dirge, 104
Discipline, 117–18
dissection of poetry, 5
Divine Comedy, The, 102, 150
Do not go gentle . . ., 155
Dobson, Austin, 153, 154, 155
Doctor Faustus, 112
Don Juan, 48, 51, 102, 152
Donne, John, 4, 28, 70, 84, 106, 123, 132, 140, 145, 151, 172, 210
Doolittle, Hilda, 162
Douglas, Keith, 156
Dover Beach, 192
dramatic lyric, 110
dramatic poetry, 108–9, 148, 177 (*see also* Shakespeare and other dramatic authors)
Drayton, Michael, 108, 109, 151, 157, 158
Dream of the Rood, The, 66
Drummond of Hawthornden, William, 70, 108, 156
Dryden, John, 70, 80, 105, 106, 107, 109, 145
Dry Salvages, The, 156
Duchess of Malfi, The, 37
Ducks, 158

Dunbar, William, 93
Dunciad, The, 82, 105
Dunn, Douglas, 197
Dylan, Bob, 213

Earl Brand, 93
eclogue, 109
Eclogues, 108
Eclogue between the Motherless, 109
Eclogue from Iceland, 108
Ecstasy, The, see *Extasie*
Edward, 98
Egg-Head, 197
elegy, 106
Elegy written in a Country Churchyard, 86, 106, 151, 172
Elegy III, 28
Eleven for a Bestiary, 110
Eliot, T. S., 4, 59, 61, 106, 109, 115, 133, 156, 162, 164, 166, 211
Elizabeth I, 157
Empson, William, 101, 155, 175
Encyclopaedia Britannica, 7
end-stopped line, 37, 177
English Bards and Scotch Reviewers, 136
English Pronouncing Dictionary, An, 20n.
enjambement, 37, 149
Enoch Arden, 108
Enright, D. J., 163, 165, 211
epic, 102
epic narrative, 103
epic simile, 143
epigram, 107
epistle, 105
Epistle to a Godson, 105
Epistle to Dr Arbuthnot, 105
Epitaph on the Death of Sir Philip Sidney, 157
Epithalamion, 97, 106
epithalamium, 106
Epithalamium made at Lincolnes Inne, 106
equivalence, theory of, 38
Esperanto, 9
Essay on Criticism, An, 45, 61, 104, 112, 149
Evangeline, 157
Evans, Dame Edith, 4, 58
Eve of Saint Agnes, 137, 152
Eve of Saint Mark, 149
Everlasting Mercy, The, 103, 149
Ewart, Gavin, 165
examinations, 3, 100, 185–9
Exstasie, The, 132
eye-rhyme, 52

fable, 104
Faerie Queene, The, 24, 47, 152
Fairground, 203
falling rhythm, 22, 23–4
feminine rhyme, 32, 46, 49, 50
Fenton, James, 84, 105
Finley, Ian Hamilton, 207
Fish, The, 201
Fitzgerald, Edward, 68, 85, 173
Flanders, Michael, 213
Fletcher, Giles, 102
Fletcher, John, 101, 109

Flint, F. S., 162
Flowers in Concrete, 207
folk-song, 87
folk-tale, 89
foot, metrical, 25–44, 195–200
formless beauty, 2
Fourteen Ways of Touching the Peter, 202–3
Fowler, H. W., 45
France, an Ode, 160
Fraser, George, 54
free verse, 159–67
French Persian Cats Having a Ball, 204
Freud, Sigmund, 114, 140
From Feathers to Iron, 196
Fry, Christopher, 109
Fuller, John, 214
Furnival, John, 207

Garden, The, 39, 135, 149
Garden of Proserpine, The, 50
Garrett, John, 87n.
Gay, John, 40, 80
Geography of the House, 209
Georgiad, The, 102
Gershon, Karen, 211
Gershwin, George, 212
Ghosts of the Buffaloes, The, 62
Gielgud, John, 4
Gilbert, W. S., 51, 55, 126
Gimson, A. C. 20n.
Glories of our blood and state, The, 180–4
Godwin, William, 114
Goeritz, Mathias, 207
Goldsmith, Oliver, 108
Gondibert, 151
Good Man in Hell, The, 123
Graves, Robert, 63, 88, 158, 203
Gray, Thomas, 86, 106, 151, 172
Green Grow the Rushes, O, 144
Greville, Fulke, Lord Brooke, 157
Grimald, Nicholas, 157
Gunn, Thomas, 201

haiku, 161, 201
half-rhyme, 53
Hamlet, 29–30, 79, 127, 139, 185
Handel, G. F., 95
Hands, 202
Hardy, Thomas, 150, 155, 158
Harvey, Gabriel, 157
Harvey, F. W., 158
Haste to the Wedding, 106
Have a Good Time, 156
H.D., 162
Headmaster, Modern Style, 210
Healthy Spot, A, 197
Heaney, Seamus, 56
Heath-Stubbs, John, 110, 156
Heir of Linne, The, 56
Hell Gate, 103
Henley, W. E., 154
Henry IV, part I, 124; part II, 126
Henryson, Robert, 104, 152
Herbert, George, 104, 115, 117–18, 138–9
here's a little mouse) and . . ., 165
heroic couplets, 24, 149

Herrick, Robert, 12, 69, 80, 108, 170
Hesperides, 108
hexameter, 26, 152, 156–7
Hiawatha, 161
His Shield, 203
Hobbs, Carleton, 58
Hobsbaum, Philip, 209
hokku, see *haiku*
Holbrook, David, 210
Hollow Men, The, 162
Holy Sonnets, 5, 151
Holy Willie's Prayer, 158
Homer, 102
Hood, Thomas, 50
Hopkins, Gerard Manley, 55, 106, 151, 155, 198–200
Horatian Ode upon Cromwell's Return from Ireland, 106
Hornpipe, 62
Horses on the Camargue, 192
Housman, A. E., 88, 103, 140
Hudibras, 50–1, 149
Hughes, Ted, 197–8, 211
Hymn to God the Father, 84–5
Hymn to Intellectual Beauty, 107
Hynd Horn, 93
hypermetric syllables, 29–30, 32–3, 36, 41, 46

I had a little Nut-tree . . ., 113
i say no words, 165
I sing of a maiden, 98
iambic, 22, 24, 26, 28–43, 46, 148–53, 156–9, 160, 177, 181, 201, 203
Idiot Boy, The, 103, 136
Idylls, 108
Idylls of the King, 24, 103
If I could tell you . . ., 155
Iliad, 102, 172
image, dominant, 7
imagery, 112, 137–47, 182
Imagists, 162, 169
imperfect rhyme, 52–7
In a Balcony, 110
In a Gondola, 110
In after days . . ., 154
In Memoriam, 146, 150
In Memory of my Father, 209
In Memory of my Grandmother, 210
In Memory of Sigmund Freud, 106
In the Wilderness, 158
In Winter Woods, 162
incantation, incantatory, 7, 161
incremental repetition, 98
internal rhyme, 65
intonation, 7, 11, 15, 74–8
inversion of feet, 32–44
Is my team ploughing?, 88
Isabella, 48, 152
Isaiah, 162

Jabberwocky, 101
Jackson, Glenda, 4
Jane Wakeful, 165
January and May, 209
Japanese influences, 200–1
Jellon Graeme, 144
Jennings, Elizabeth, 210, 211
Jerusalem, 144
Job, 162
John Gilpin, 103
Johnson, Samuel, 104, 129, 149, 175

Jones, David, 164
Jones, Daniel, 20n.
Journey of the Magi, 166
Jung, Carl, 114

Kairos and Logos, 156
Keats, John, 47, 48, 107, 127, 137, 140, 149, 152, 171, 172, 183
Ke-bonk, ke-bonk fallacy, 15, 17, 28, 33, 42
Keen Edge, The, 208
Keyes, Sidney, 128
King, Henry, 159
King Lear, 139, 142, 170
Kipling, Rudyard, 97, 150
Kirkup, James, 140
Krylov, Ivan A., 104
Kubla Khan, 69, 101, 125

La Fontaine, Jean de, 104
Lady Chatterley's Lover, 208
Lak of Stedfastness, 153
L'Allegro, 70
Lady of Shalott, The, 158
lament, 106
Lament for the Makaris, 93
Lament for Philip Sparrow, The, 158
Lamia, 47
Landor, Walter Savage, 131
Langland, William, 66
Larkin, Philip, 187, 209, 210, 211
Last Confession, A, 110
Last of the Flock, The, 103
Lawrence, D. H., 162
Lepanto, 97
Letter addressed to the Corpse of Eliot, 106
Letter to Lord Byron, 105, 152
Letter to Maria Gisborne, 105
Levi, Peter, 56–7, 152
Lewis, Cecil Day, 103, 104, 107, 140, 169, 196, 199
Lie, The, 82
light rhyme, 55
limerick, 25
Lindsay, Vachel, 62, 94
logical sequence, 2, 7, 112–23
long measure, 150
Longfellow, Henry Wadsworth, 157, 161
Long Trail, The, 95n. (anthology)
Long Trail, The (Kipling), 97
Lord Randal, 98
Lotos-Eaters, The, 60
Love, 138–9
Lovelace, Richard, 126
Lowell, Amy, 162
Lowell, Robert, 210
Lycidas, 106
Lyke-Wake Dirge, The, 91, 95
lyric, 48, 107, 113, 167
Lyrical Ballads, 103

Macbeth, 100, 127, 129, 139, 209
Macbeth, George, 62, 104, 110, 165, 166, 201, 209, 211
MacCaig, Norman, 165
MacDiarmid, Hugh, 162
McGough, Roger, 165, 205
Maclean, Alasdair, 162, 209
MacLeish, Archibald, 55

MacNeice, Louis, 54, 104, 109, 129n., 187, 188n., 199
MacPherson, James, 162
McTell, Ralph, 213
macron, 18, 22
madrigal, 48–9, 213
magic, 89–90
Maiden in the moor lay . . ., 144
Manual of English Prosody, 39
Mariana, 60, 96
Marlowe, Christopher, 36, 109, 112, 175
Marmion, 47, 149
Marquis, Don, 165
Marvell, Andrew, 39, 106, 130, 135, 149
Marx, Karl, 114
masculine rhyme, 45–6, 50
Masefield, John, 103, 149
May Queen, The, 167
Meditations of an Old Woman, 162
Memoirs of Uncle Harry, The, 166
Merciles Beaute, 154
Meredith, George, 151
Merlin and Vivien, 60–1
Messiah, The, 95
metaphysical poetry, 123, 145
metre, 17–44, 148–59
Michael, 108, 172
Middle English, 66
Midsummer Night's Dream, A, 65, 74, 141–2
Milk for the Cat, 4
Milligan, Spike, 213
Milton (Blake), 102
Milton, John, 8, 9–10, 15, 22, 70, 71–2, 102, 106, 108, 114, 132, 145, 148, 151, 163, 170, 193, 213
missing dates, 155
Mr Sludge, the 'Medium', 110
Mrs Robinson and Mr Smith, 103–4
Mitchell, Adrian, 105, 205
Mitchell, Joni, 213
mock epic, 102
Modern Love, 151
Monologue of a Fat Man, 209
monometer, 26
Monro, Harold, 4
Moore, Marianne, 201–3
Morall Fabillis, 104
Morgan, Edwin, 62, 165, 166, 204–5
Morgante, 102
Morris, William, 96
Morte D' Arthur, 195
Mosaic for Marianne Moore, A, 202
mosaic rhyme, 56
Moses, Anna Mary ('Grandma'), 190
Much Ado about Nothing, 35, 51
Muir, Edwin, 106, 123, 150
Municipal Gallery Revisited, The, 152
Mushrooms, 161
music and poetry, 34, 167
My Last Duchess, 110, 192
Myth, The, 123

Nabara, 103
narrative verse, 47, 112, 152
Nash, Ogden, 165

Nashe, John, 138, 143
Nephelidia, 73
Never weather-beaten sail, 99
New Cambridge Bibliography of English Literature, 66n.
New Year Letter, 149
Nicholson, Norman, 165
Noah's Journey, 211
Nosce Teipsum, 104
notation for rhyme-schemes, 47
notation for rhythm, 18
Nott, Kathleen, 56
Novák, Ladislav, 207
Noyes, Alfred, 167
Nutbrown Maid, The, 109
Nymphidia, 158

O Rose, thou art sick!, 43
O ruddier than the cherry . . ., 40
occasional verse, 105–6
octosyllabics, 149
ode, 106–7
Ode for Saint Cecilia's Day, 107
Ode on a Grecian Urn, 183
Ode on the Death of the Duke of Wellington, 107
Ode on the Morning of Christ's Nativity, 9–10, 170
Ode to Duty, 107
Ode to Fear, 107
Ode to a Nightingale, 107
Ode to the West Wind, 107, 150
Odyssey, 102
Old English, 66, 176
Old Fools, The, 209
Old MacDonald had a farm, 58, 94
Olivier, Sir Laurence, 58
On a Deserted Shore, 214
On a Fan, 153
On a Raised Beach, 162
On Catullus, 131
On English Poetry, 63
On the New Forcers of Conscience . . ., 151
onomatopoeia, 5, 58–64, 67, 168
Open Day at Porton, 105
Open Letter to Richard Crossman, 105
Operation, The, 210
Orchestra, 104
Orgy, 204
Original Sin, 54
Ossian, 162
Othello, 17, 35, 129, 139, 173
ottava rima, 152
Otway, Thomas, 142
Owen, Wilfred, 53, 135
Oxford Book of Carols, The, 94
Oxford Book of Sixteenth Century Verse, 157

paeon, 198–9
Paradise Illustrated, 163
Paradise Lost, 24, 35, 101, 102, 105, 148, 163, 200
Paradise Regained, 102
pararhyme, 53
paraphrase, 112, 193
Partridge, Eric, 95n.
Passion, 150
Passionate Shepherd to his Love, The, 175–80
pastoral, 108, 109, 177–80
Pastoral Elegy, A, 108

Patience, 126
Patmore, Coventry, 158
Pavan for an Unborn Infanta, 165
Paxton, Tom, 213
Peaceable Kingdom, The, 162
pentameter, 26, 28–39, 148–51, 160
Pericles, 170
phonetic form, 15
phonetics, 52
Phonetics, 22n.
Phyllis, 157
Picasso, Pablo, 160
Pied Beauty, 151
Pillar of Fame, The, 12
Pilling, Christopher, 55
Plath, Sylvia, 62, 161, 210
Poe, Edgar Allan, 72, 141
Poem in October, 203
Poet's Tongue, The, 87n.
Poetry Olympics, 212
Polyolbion, 157
polysyllabic rhyme, 46, 51
Pope, Alexander, 45, 52, 61, 82, 102, 104, 105, 112, 140, 145, 149, 172, 189
Porter, Cole, 212
Porter, Peter, 151
Poulter's Measure, 156–7
Pound, Ezra, 101, 115, 154, 156, 162, 164, 211
Practical Phonetics, 22n.
Preface to Shakespeare, 175
Prelude, The, 140, 148, 171, 200
Pre-Raphaelites, 126
Press, John, 110, 209, 210
Prince Athanase, 150
Prioress's Tale, The, 103
Prisoner of Chillon, The, 47, 149
Private Ortheris's Song, 97
Proctor, Thomas, 82
Prometheus Unbound, 108, 168
Prophecy of Dante, The, 150
Prothalamion, 46–7, 106
proverbs, 67
Psalms, 162
Pulci, Luigi, 102
Puttenham, George, 12
Pygmalion, 67
Pyrrhic, 25

quadruple rhyme, 46
quantitative verse, 21–2, 157, 204
quantity, 21, 157, 195
quatrain, 150–5, 166, 177, 181

radio, 109, 186, 211
Radio Times, 213
Raine, Kathleen, 149, 187, 214
Raleigh, Sir Walter, 82, 179
Rape of Lucrece, The, 103, 152
Rape of the Lock, The, 102
Raven, The, 72
Read, Sir Herbert, 141
reading aloud, 4, 11, 14, 15–16, 186
recitation, 58–9, 186
Recurrence, The, 123
Red, red rose, A, 137–8
Redemption, 115–16
Redgrove, Peter, 162
Refrain, 92–9, 153–4
Remembrance Day, 158
repetition, 7, 15, 65, 79–99, 100, 155, 161

Revolt of Islam, The, 48, 152
Reward, His, 13, 14
rhyme, 7, 18, 45–57, 79, 100, 148–59, 160, 167, 168, 181
rhyme royal, 152
rhythm, 7, 15, 17–44, 79, 100, 148–59, 168, 195–204
Riddling Knight, The, 93, 144
Ridler, Anne, 103, 109, 165, 187, 190n., 211
Riflemen Form, 82
Rime Couée, 157
Ring, The, 150
Ring out, you bells. . ., 120
rising rhythm, 22
ritual, 7, 89–91, 93, 161
Roberts, Michael, 155
Rodgers, W. R., 199
Roethke, Theodore, 162
Romantic revival, 145
Romeo and Juliet, 34–5, 51, 128
rondeau, 153
rondel, 154
rondelet, 154
roundel, 154
Roundel is wrought, A, 154
Rosselson, Leon, 213
Rossetti, Christina, 83, 158
Rove-over foot, 198–9
Rubáiyát of Omar Khayyám, 68, 85, 151, 172–3
Rugby Chapel, 161
Ruth, 158

Saint Simeon Stylites, 110
Saintsbury, George, 39
Salmon Fisher to the Salmon, The, 56
Samson Agonistes, 108
Sanitized Sonnets, The, 151
Santa Fé Trail, The, 62
Satire, 105, 112, 136, 149
Scannell, Vernon, 104, 110, 158, 187, 189, 209, 211
Scissor Man, 110
School's Out, 25
Scot, Michael, 153
Scott, Sir Walter, 47, 69, 83, 149, 186
Sea and the Mirror, The, 97–8
Sea Surface Full of Clouds, 101
Seat for Three, A, 154
Sensitive Plant, The, 47
septenarius, 26
sestet, 151, 158
sestina, 156, 204
Sestina: A Consolation, 158
Sestina: Altaforte, 156
Sextains, 156
Sexton, Anne, 189, 210
Shakespeare, William, 17, 22, 24, 28, 33, 36–7, 52, 65, 69, 79, 80–1, 100, 103, 109, 114, 116, 120, 122, 124, 127, 128, 129, 132, 138, 151, 152, 160, 170, 173, 185, 210
Shall I compare thee . . ., 101
shaped poems, 12–13
Shaw, G. B., 67, 140
She is not fair to outward view . . ., 119
Shelley, Percy Bysshe, 47, 48, 85, 105, 106, 107, 108, 109, 131–2, 138, 139, 140, 141, 150, 152, 168, 189
Shepheard's Calender, The, 65, 108

Shepherd's Garland, The, 108, 109
Shirley, James, 127, 180
Shooting of his Dear, 103
short measure, 150
Shorts, 148
Shower, The, 122–3
Sidney, Sir Philip, 22, 70, 108, 109, 120, 151, 157
Silver Wedding, 209
Simias, 13
Sir Beelzebub, 62
Sitwell, Edith, 61, 62, 101, 106, 191–2
Skeat, W. W., 155
Skelton, John, 83, 158
Skelton, Robin, 89n., 110, 187
Skeltonics, 158
slant rhyme, 53
Smart, Christopher, 67
Sohrab and Rustum, 103
Solt, Mary Ellen, 207
Song of the Devil, 210
Song of Myself, 162
Song of Solomon, 162
Song to David, A, 67–8
sonnet, 24, 151, 166, 204
sonnet, tailed, 151
Sonnets from the Portuguese, 151
sound and sense, 11
Spellcraft, 89n.
Spender, Stephen, 169, 192, 199
Spenser, Edmund, 22, 46–7, 52, 65, 97, 102, 106, 108, 141, 151, 152
Spenserian stanza, 152, 164
Spinster's Sweet-Arts, The, 110
spondee, 25, 26
spring! may, 165
Sprung Rhythm, 198–200
Squire, Sir John, 96n.
Starlings in George Square, The, 110
Stevens, Wallace, 101
Stone-Age Woman, 110
Strange Meeting, 53
Streets of London, The, 213
stress, 18–44, 161, 195
Structure of Complex Words, The, 175
substitution, theory of, 38
Suckling, Sir John, 75
Sullivan, Arthur, 126
Surrealism, 114
Surrey, Henry Howard, Earl of, 118
Swann, Donald, 213
Swinburne, Algernon Charles, 13–14, 50, 72–3, 82, 140, 141, 152, 154–5
syllabic verse, 195, 200–3
synthetic rhyme, 55

tailed rhyme, 157, 204
Taill of the Uponlandis Mous . . ., 152
Tale of Sir Thopas, 158
Tarantella, 158
Task, The, 148
television, 186, 241
Tempest, The, 97, 200
Tennyson, Alfred, 22, 41–2, 59–61, 69, 82, 96, 103, 107, 108, 109, 110, 146, 149, 150, 158, 172, 195

Terza Rima, 150
Testament of Beauty, The, 157
tetrameter, 26, 40, 42, 149, 153, 158, 161, 177, 181
Thackray, Jake, 213
That Daughter of Debate, 157
Theocritus, 108
This is the Key of the Kingdom, 144–5
This be the verse, 210
Thomas, Edward, 158
Thomas, Dylan, 12, 59, 61, 103, 155, 199, 203
Thomasine, 108
Thorn, The, 103
Those Childish Fears, 158
Thoughts out of Doors, 152
Three Mirrors, The, 123
Three Poems of the Atomic Bomb, 106
Three Poor Witches, 62
To ——, 131–2
To Ann Scott-Moncrieff, 106
To Anthea, who may Command him Anything, 69
To a Louse, 158
To a Mouse, 158
To the Body, 158
To the Unco Guid, 76–7
To Walter de la Mare, 106
Tomb of David Hume, The, 166
Tomlinson, Charles, 162
Tom's Garland, 151
Tourneur, Cyril, 109
Traill, Henry Duff, 96
Trampwoman's Tragedy, A, 158
Trimeter, 26, 42, 158
Trio for Two Cats and a Trombone, 62
triolet, 155
triple rhyme, 46
triplets, 149
trisyllabic rhyme, 46
Triumph of Life, The, 150
trochaic, 22, 23, 26, 46, 161, 201
trochee, 26, 40–1, 203
Troilus and Criseyde, 152
Troilus stanza, 152
True Story, A, 201
Truelove, A, 157
Tunning of Elinor Rumming, The, 158
Twelfth Night, 35
Two Sonnets (G. S. Fraser), 54
Two Voices, The, 149

Ulysses (Tennyson), 60, 69
Ulysses and the Siren, 110
unaccented rhyme, 54–5
Unexploded Bomb, The, 104

Vanity of Human Wishes, The, 104, 149
Vaughan, Henry, 122–3
Veld Eclogue, 149
Venice Preserved, 142
Venus and Adonis, 103
verse drama, 108–9
verse essay, 104
Victor, 103
villanelle, 155
Villanelle, 155
Villanelle for Harpo Marx, 155
Villanelle of Sunlight, 156
Villon, François, 153, 154

Virgil, 102, 108
Vision and Prayer, 12
Vision of Piers Plowman, The, 66
visual form, 11–14
Voice of Authority, The, 156

Wain, John, 155–6
Waller, Edmund, 77
Waring, 158
Warren, Robert Penn, 54
Waste Land, The, 164, 166, 211
Weathers, 158
Webster, John, 37, 109, 128
Wells, J. C., 22n.
Welsh Incident, 203
What, no perdy!, 154
What the Chairman Told Tom, 163
When I saw you last, Rose . . ., 155
When the Lamp is shattered . . ., 138
When to her lute Corinna sings . . ., 49
White Devil, The, 128
Whitman, Walt, 141, 162
Wilde, Oscar, 85, 103
Wild Old Wicked Man, The, 96
Wilderness, The, 128
Willow-wren and the Stare, The, 97
Wind's Bastinado, The, 62
Winter's Tale, The, 35
Wishes for his Supposed Mistress, 138
Witnesses, The, 158
Woddis, Roger, 213
Words, 158
Words for Music Perhaps, 96
Wordsworth, William, 103, 107, 108, 109, 114, 136, 140, 148, 158, 160, 171–2, 189
Wyatt, Sir Thomas, 14, 154

Yeats, William Butler, 96, 110, 140, 152, 160
You are the town . . ., 158
Young British Soldier, The, 97
Young Women in Rollers, 197